Weep and Wail

A Compilation of Verse
and Prose
By Lisa Talbott

With Commentary by
Michael Paul Hurd

i

ISBN (paperback):

Publisher (paperback): Independently Published via Amazon by Lineage Independent Publishing, Marriottsville, MD

e-book: Independently Published by Lineage Independent Publishing, Marriottsville, MD

Maryland (USA) Sales and Use Tax Entity: Lineage Independent Publishing, Marriottsville, MD 21104

www.lineage-publishing.com

lineagepublishing@gmail.com

Other works by Lisa Talbott:

Pen and Inks

Available from Online Booksellers

Other works by Michael Paul Hurd:

Lineage: A Novel

Soldier, Citizen, Settler: Lineage Series, Book Two

Iniquity and Retribution: Lineage Series, Book Three

Wayward Son: Lineage Series, Book Four

Available from Online Booksellers

Contents

About the Title

"Weep and Wail" has its origins in Cockney rhyming slang. Used in London's East End since the early 19th Century, it is more than just a rhyming association; rather, the slang phrase reflects the meaning of the expression itself. Consider "plates of meat." In Cockney slang, it means "feet," derived from how a market hawker's feet felt at the end of a long day plying his or her wares. In true rhyming slang tradition, it might sometimes be expressed merely by the first word, "plates." Add to that a colorful phrase like "Khyber Pass," meaning "ass" (or "arse") and you could politely tell someone to be on their way or risk "a plate up the Khyber."

The phrase "Weep and Wail" is used exclusively to describe a tale, and more definitively a "beggar's tale." Lisa chose this as the title for her second book because it reflects what a poet's life could be: a beggar's tale – especially if the poetry does not find an audience.

Introduction
By Michael Paul Hurd

I first came across Lisa Talbott's poetry as I was preparing my third historical fiction novel, "Iniquity and Retribution: Lineage Series, Book Three" for release. One of my "signature" techniques in my books is to include an epigraph as a separator between each chapter, usually a quotation that relates to the theme of what follows. I don't remember exactly how I came across it, but one of Lisa's recently written poems was a perfect fit. In fact, the fit was so perfect that I wanted to replace another quotation already laid down in the book with Lisa's poem.

Taking the bull by the horns, I reached out to Lisa through social media and explained to her what I was trying to do. One thing led to another, and I ultimately got permission to include the poem, "Our Last Dance" in my book. That initial contact has led to a continuing electronic friendship that has expanded to include Lisa's mother, Elizabeth, as well. I also included another of Lisa's poems in my fourth book, "Wayward Son: Lineage Series, Book Four," and look forward to finding another of her poems for inclusion in my next book, with a working title of "The Seventh Wife: Lineage Series, Book Five."

In the interest of full disclosure, rarely have I focused on reading poetry as a literary genre'. I prefer narrative prose and especially historical fiction. In fact, I have not personally paid much attention to poetry since my early college days and undergraduate literature courses. Lisa changed that. I now find myself reading not only Lisa's work but that of other emerging poets as well.

Lisa and Elizabeth were part of my pre-release team for Books Three and Four and will be part of that team again for Book Five, which is being written concurrently with this anthology of Lisa's work. What is even more notable is that Lisa and I have never met face-to-face. She is in Portugal, having retired from the UK to her "place in the sun." I am in Maryland, in the United States, having also recently retired myself. I did, however, spend over a decade living and working in the United Kingdom – which made it even easier for me to understand some of the "Brit-speak" in Lisa's works. I've also kept the preferred British spellings throughout, as I felt it would be a disservice to Lisa to "Americanize" them.

Lisa's first compilation, "Pen and Inks," with illustrations by Lucas Volaart-Vermeulen, was published in 2019 and remains available on Amazon and Barnes and Noble in both printed and electronic formats. Her poems in both books are at times evocative, humorous, often poignant, and at other times, as they say in England, "quite cheeky." Some may be based on real life, but the majority are, as Lisa puts it, "just a figment of my wild imagination." You be the judge of which is which.

I originally thought that this compilation would be simply a volume of Lisa's poetic works, without regard for structure. Instead, I made the editorial decision (with Lisa's concurrence, of course!) to group her poems into thematic categories as reflected in the Table of Contents. Then, as we were laying down the final verses for the book, Lisa tells me that she has written several short stories as well. I couldn't resist including five of them – they are just as good as her poetry!

Part One: Life... In General

From the homeless man on the street corner to the Queen in Buckingham Palace and everything in between, the observations Lisa makes about the generalities of life range from the humorous to the provocative. In fact, one of the poems could, with a little imagination, possibly be set to the melody from a well-known play by George Bernard Shaw. I'll leave you guessing as to which one and which song.

There are places in the next poems where an American reader might not understand the terminology. For example, a "10 tog duvet" is a comforter that is suitable for the cooler nights of spring or autumn. A winter-weight duvet/comforter would have a "tog" rating of 12 or higher. The "tog" as a unit of thermal measurement was invented by the Shirley Institute in Manchester, England, during the 1940s.

Elsewhere, references to food might be baffling to anyone who did not enjoy a proper British upbringing. Take "chip buttie" for example. It's basically a "French fry sandwich." However, I have it on good authority (my wife, whose mother is British) that there is really nothing tastier than a chip buttie made with fresh bread, creamery butter, and piping-hot chips/fries. The butter melts into the bread, coats the chips, and teases the palate... Simple, but exquisite!

We are certainly fortunate that Lisa's works, even with cultural variations, are more coherent and understandable than Lewis Carroll's famous poem, "Jabberwocky."

" *'Twas brillig and the slythy toves*

Did gyre and gymble in the wabe

All mimsy were the borogroves

And the mome raths outgrabe."

"The curtain twitcher"

The window cleaner's on his way; hasn't been for weeks:
Tried to do 'em by myself but can't see through the streaks.
They're full of flies and nicotine and fingerprints galore.
I have to get this 'man that can' cos I can't reach no more.

Don't think that I'm a gossip or a nosey so-and-so.
I like to keep abreast of where my neighbours come and go.
It's purely out of interest, see. Neighbourly, you'd say.
And I sit here just to 'people watch'; hours and hours a day.

Oh the stories I could tell you all, but like I said before,
I'm not about to gossip therefore nought will pass my door.
But I like to write about my 'friends', a 'tribute' may say I?
Pages in my journal. My legacy when I die.

None so blind and deaf as those who do not wish to know.
But cruelty such as I've been dealt has been a bitter blow.
Oh I know the names they call me. It's why I stay inside.
Safe behind these lonely walls and dingy nets I hide.

My journal's for the cleaner. He's the kindest man around.
Photos, deeds, bonds and shares: all are leather-bound.
I'll leave it on my doorstep, with the payment he is due.
Cos he's the son that I gave up… I guess it's time he knew!

"Summer"

"You've got a pool, you lucky thing".
On days like this I tiptoe in.
Warm at first, then deeper, colder.
Belly-flop, like a human boulder.

Inhale an' gasp in shock / delight!
my ten stone blubber's weightless; right?
I walk a length. I swim a breadth;
Panting, wheezing, out of breath.

It really is insanely hot,
I'm melting here; I kid you not.
My swimming pool, whilst might seem chic,
looks something like an oil slick!

My Factor 50's washed away,
exposing flesh to burn today.
No longer glam or Instagram-cool.
A 'drowned-rat' in my swimming pool.

Strap lines, blisters, chlorine-hair.
Stretch marks match my silverware.
Mozzie bites that itch and swell.
Damn Cystitis' back as well.

The wasps are out - got stung last night,
I stink of putrid 'after-bite'.
My sheets smell too, they wreak of sweat,
I can't be arsed to change them yet.

Don't get me wrong, I love the sun,
but summer's kinder on the young.
I pray each day to Mighty Thor
so I don't have to 'wax' no more.

See, autumn now's a blink away.
Yippee for my 10 tog duvet.
No doubt in weeks I'll curse the rain
and yearn the sizzling heat again.

"Just a normal day"

I'm going shopping in the morning.
Trying to get there after nine.
It might seem catastrophic but I'm OUT of gin and tonic
and I hope when I get back I'll still be fine!

Well I drove right up to Intermarché car park.
No car nor bike or four-by-four was there.
Is it Easter Sunday, or another public funday?
I need toilet rolls, and shampoo for my hair.

So off I drove to Lidl feeling certain,
they'll be people queueing outside the door.
No need to feel such harry cos it's much like cash 'n carry
and I got all that I needed, and much more.

Petrol next, I'm running almost empty.
Self service here is not y'normal thing.
There's Carlos at the garage who fills up my Clio carriage
and he thrusts the nozzle very firmly in!

Satiated both my car and booty.

Homeward bound, I'll see these next weeks through.

The sun here's shining brightly, I thank God I'm not in Blighty,

so I'll adios, au revoir, and toodle-do.

"Sorry . . . ma"

Dear folks I'm at the station. (No, not the bus or train!)
'Policeman Plod' arrested me. I'm mortified with shame.

I took my mother shopping cos she needed Dentafix.
Loo rolls too she's also got horrendous direa, dyer-ear,
dihorrea . .
She's also got the shits!

I pulled into the car park but she's desp'rate for the loo.
So I detoured to the subway fed the meter a quid or two.

No way I'm going in there! I'll just wait here, outside.
Piss and vomit, weed and filth - disgust is amplified.

Well mum's been gone for ages! Many came and went.
And I'm stood like a lemon, (a useless ornament!)

Leaning on the handrail with my cigarette alight.
Policeman Plod approached me asking "everything
alright?"

© 2020 Lisa Talbott

I can't believe he disbelieved the story I relayed!

He claimed I was soliciting! At my age? Sir behave!

I'm being kept here overnight and just allowed one call.

I tried to call my sister but she's out! Goddammit all.

My poor decrepit lovely mum. A wicked, sad calamity!

I'll not get out 'til morning . . and she's stuck in the lavatory!

"The boxer"

I've always liked the boxing, on TV or a show.
My dad was a well-known boxer - years and years ago.

I remember as a youngster how he'd train for hours on end.
And sometimes he pulled muscles that our mum would
have to tend.

He used to wrap crepe bandages around his hands and
fingers
underneath his boxing gloves. God how the memory
lingers!

The punch bag and the skipping rope. The miles he used to
run.
To me, a kid, it seemed hard work; to dad it was all for fun.

He always wore a pure white vest when fighting in the ring.
Satin shorts (all par the course), so proud my heart would
sing.

Always at the working clubs these boxing do's took place
and even after all these years I STILL can smell that place.

The sweat, the toil, the passion. The boxers; trainers too.
Adrenalin from the ringside. The shouts of the 'well-to-do'.

He won the County Championship. He'd never lost a fight.
Was well renowned in Leicestershire: and then turned Pro
one night.

The City Hall was heaving. Never prouder, have I felt.
But the guy was fast, my dad outclassed, and LOST that
Lonsdale Belt.

We got chips from our local chippie, walking home in the
dark and damp.
And mum took loads of photos of us kids, with dad. OUR
champ!

"Dear Majesty"

I just LOVE the royal family. I'm a royalist; through and
through.
Their thrills and spills and scandals are entwined in our
lives too.

They're only 'normal' people (oh, albeit with blue blood).
I wish they lived next door to me, or at least our
neighbourhood.

I'd take round home-grown veggies; or fruits picked from
our trees.
I'd curtesy low before them, down on bended knees.

I'd have them round for coffee. And yes, I'll bake some
cakes.
(I'll have to practise weeks before to counteract mistakes.)

I'd have to blast my place first though, make sure my
toilet's clean.
(I'm really fond of curries so you'll all know what I mean!)

I'd cringe if 'one' found cat hairs on a chair I'd sat 'em on.
This rubbish from Ikea I've got is nothing like a Throne!

I'd love to get to know them cos I'm sure they'd gel with
me.
Could even use our swimming pool, we're private here you
see!

I could take them to my local for a glass of home-made red.
(On second thoughts it's lethal, so p'haps a beer instead?)

Oh I'd love to have the royals here to be my special guests.
The freedom of obscurity, paparazzi, bullet-proof vests.

Diana's dashing Princes with their wives, and babes in
arms,
all welcome here to stay, indeed the entire entourage.

And should there be too many and we're running out of
beds,
we've a whopping great big garage, and two really comfy
sheds.

So Ma'am, if YOU should ever feel inclined to bring your
family,
Get a flight, rent a car, and holiday here with me.

"Airbrush Windrush!"

A Lady moved in to next door,
sometime around '64.
She was different from me cos her skin was like tea.
The likes never seen here before.

She held her head high when she'd walk.
The opposite of me (cheese and chalk?).
She thought me a nerd, cos I'd never heard
Caribbean patois talk!

I was in awe of this lady, you'd say.
The Motown music she'd play!
It sounded so neat, I would groove to the beat
and I'd steal round her house every day.

The smells from her kitchen . . . divine!
Her food I can still bring to mind.
Ackee and dumplings, coconut rice puddings.
Jamaican Rum always, not wine.

She frequented our chapel in Stroud.
Knew all of our hymns, and sang loud.
The whole congregation, without dispensation,
cringed with their consciences bowed.

But Nurse Hyatt won't be reimbursed
for her skin, which her work colleagues cursed.
She endured indignation (with proud resignation)
much more than the 'loonies' she nursed.

Then last year my neighbour was gone!
The Home Office forced her along.
The Windrush had brought her, but let's now deport her.
Good grief, how the 'System' went wrong!

Families in turmoil and strife!
Talk about 'twisting the knife'.
Kids broken hearted, generations were parted,
and made to begin a new life.

Our community was never the same.
That lady left MORE than her name.
"Love thy neighbour, creed or colour"
May the Home Office ever feel shame!

"Sampling glamping"

I'd never been camping before . . .
(preferring more comfy resorts).
But pensions had not been too fruitful,
so opted for tents. . . of a sort.

A Yurt's not a tent? Then forgive me!
. . . being the heathen I am.
But surely if it's made out of canvas
it's a hippy-home: made to sound glam?

I arrived at the 'glampsite' in darkness:
It rained, yet I came here for sun!
I foresee that this break's gonna kill me.
But I'm steadfast in making it fun.

The site was indeed quite luxurious.
(Tho' course not the Ritz, or the Grand.)
There's yoga, pilates, and reiki,
and we'll eat off the fat of the land.

They're bohemian-type people, the owners,
(who look like they're fresh off the Ark)
the women wear long floral dresses.
The guys leave a BIG question mark.

We harvested grapes and the olives.
Gathered eggs from the hens in the coop.
I declined on the last invitation,
to partake in a wild boar shoot!

But the boar must've sensed my displeasure
'cos I heard the beast snuffling, real close.
Out of all the damn Yurts on this haven,
it was mine that the hairy brute chose!

Well I leapt out that flap in the canvas,
squealing, in pure girlie fright.
Slipped on the steps of the decking . .
and landed in something like shite!

My panic roused others to surface.
An old chap, of eighty-plus years.
He calmed me with brandy and orange,
and laughed at my outburst of fears.

The snuffling I thought was a monster?
Such trepidation of mine!
Neither boar, neither dogs, neither foxes.
But fornicators pissed up on wine!

Aw to hell with the trials of 'glamping'.
Give me white sands and blue sea!
Take me to beautiful Bali
where Ketut will be waiting for me.

"My silicone grandchild"

Don't let your kids on your iPad.
In fact . . don't even have kids at all!
Why did I not take precautions?
Mine drive me well up the wall.

They want what my 'social' can't buy them,
They yearn for designer 'glad rags'.
They refuse to come with me to 'boot sales'
wanting Gucci, not Primark price tags.

How I wish I could turn all the clocks back.
Relive adolescence again.
I'd walk the same path as my auntie,
and stay ruddy clear of all men!

I digress. . .
My daughter's a right little know-all.
The internet, her latest forté.
She pretends she's a millionaire's daughter,
and loves to go browsing eBay.

She's mad on these dolls, real life-like.
Been hankering, nigh on a year.
Then she bid on this silicone baby!
And boy did she get a thick ear.

12 hundred quid for a dolly!
(I could sell all of my kids for much less!)
I'll be glad when they're older and working
and leave me to build their own nests.

So if you see my sweet girl with a 'baby',
please do not scoff, or make fun.
Tis only a silicone dolly,
(My daughter is nowt like her mum!)

"Leavin' Blighty"

I want to go on holiday and I want to go right now!
I don't care how I get there or with who or where or how.

I want a warm location, away from Brexit stress.
Sandy beaches, clear blue sea (nothing like Skegness!)

Palm trees, leis, and cocktails. A beach hut on the sand.
Don't do villas (nor hotels). I want a no-man's Land.

I'm seeking isolation out of reach the madding crowd.
A place where I can 'find myself'; where kids are not
allowed.

I've stacks of glossy brochures on the backseat of my car.
I fantasise exclusion and in finding Shangri-la.

Then I found it! Devon Island, Canada's Baffin Bay.
(I'd had it on my Bucket List to visit there one day)

I can see it all before me, live out my fantasy.
No car to drive, no lawn to mow, no wifi or TV.
. . .
Well be careful what you wish for cos I got all that and
more!
I'd never been as cold or scared as ever been before!

I arrived there in their autumn cos was given duff advice!
'course I'd taken burning creams; for sunburn, not for ice!

Devon Island's really barren, there is NOTHING there at
all!
My beachwear, shorts and tee-shirts aren't designed for
cold at all!

Thank GOD for expedition crews . . in my hour of need!
They packed me off to Lombok where salvation's
guaranteed.

Now this, my friends, is Paradise. Picture postcard true.
Stick your Brexit where the sun don't shine I'm here for a
year or two.

"High School Reunion"

It must've been a twenty past a quarter something blurrrr.
I'm sure it was just after I'd a vodka, three, or four.
So maybe it was ten o'clock; I haven't got a clue.
But one thing is dead certain folk, we won't forget that 'do'!

There was Bazzer, Daz, and Gazza from the Agar Nook
Estates.
(You bet your bottom dollar, though, they're still the best
o'mates.)
Hey Jane my chubby buddy, can't believe you got so fat.
And Winston, gotta tell ya, you look mental in that hat.

So we're here at our reunion an' the bar's been open hours.
We'd all been reminiscing 'bout the lives and times of ours.
Seems Simon's not as simple as he was back in the day.
But Kenny IS still gorgeous (so he tells us, anyway!)

Well the dance floor was a'buzzin' with the kids of
Newbridge High.
Then Winston's passing packages, per chance to get us
high.
But Palmer (who's a copper now) had a 'dickey fit'.
Dealing 'stuff' to his old chums is not in his remit.

He tried to intervene amidst the Resurrection Shuffle
but fisty-cuffs broke out an' thus evolved a huge kerfuffle!
Palmer called for back-up from his boys down at the Nick
and that's when Jane decided she felt very very sick.

Now Billy Reid and Tinker Shaw (arch enemies back then)
tried to be all macho and forgot that they're now men!
Billy swung for Palmer as he'd done so, years before.
Then Tinker put the boot in whilst he's prostrate on the
floor.

The place was utter shambles, but the disco carried on.
Some teenage lovebirds reminiscing, smooching to 'their
song'
Till Fletcher took a hydrant and he sprayed the whole damn
place.
I decided in that moment to retreat with subtle grace.

So I called my dad, to take us home, as daughters always
do.
And Jane was wretching, throwing up, so took her with me
too.
Cos dad is of the old school, who were proper gentlemen.
They partied, danced and drank, of course, but never
caused mayhem.

My dad was in his jim-jams, whilst he waited there,
outside.
And Jane and I fell in his car, so glad for this free ride.
No lectures, scowls, or questions. He left everything
unsaid.
Hours later he brought Jane an' me, beans an' toast, in bed!

"The fawn"

The hunting season's just begun.
Already cleaned and oiled his gun.
He'll teach his young boy all he can.
(Now old enough to be a man.)

The forest's dark and damp and vast.
A target walks in view, at last.
A sweet-faced deer with haunting eyes.
Just one shot to bag the prize.

"Hush my son, lay on the ground,
crouch down low, don't make a sound".
The boy lies low and hides his face
but hears and feels his young heart race.

His father lifts his gun and aims.
The boy abhors these adult games.
He 'plays' with these that roam the land,
Why can't father understand?

The shot rings out, it echos loud.
The youngster sobs and flails about.
A thud a crash, then all is still.
A winter's pantry in one kill.

He laughed out loud, he felt elated.
Pride and manhood elevated.
And then he stops in shame and fright:
the doe's young buck appeared in sight.

He cannot kill again, this prey
so shoo's the young fawn on its way.
All too late, the damage done.
Nothing could appease his son.

'Twas 50 years ago, that day,
the boy just upped and ran away.
He lives, it's said, in forests near.
Protecting God's majestic deer.

So should you hear a rutting call,
it's just his ploy, his wherewithal
to lure the hunters far away
let nature breathe and wildlife play.

"Broken"

Broken, used and abused.
Tossed to the side like refuse.
Misplaced trust through greed and lust,
self esteem reduced to dust.

Show me your heart if you DO care.
Lend me a hand, if you dare.
Turning tack was a knife in my back.
Help me get my life on track.

Homeless. Hungry. Freezing.
Shivering. Coughing. Sneezing.
Folk pass by never give a damn why.
Piss on me. Torment me. Laugh when I cry.

Broken. Vilified. Misused.
Crazy. Demented. A screw loose.
This needle's my friend. My pain it will mend.
Now I'll fly free and sleep to my end.

"The Bad Samaritan"
A Short Story

I swore it was going to be the very last time. In fact I recall swearing it was going to be the last time, the last time! But she's my best friend.

I can't believe I'm surprised though. Ever since we were both at High School, Laura had been terrible managing her pocket money, invariably 'borrowing' from me until she could pay me back. Invariably she couldn't. Or wouldn't? but she didn't. Was it because Laura looked like I wish I did? She had the prettiest face in our class, and she knew it. Heads would turn when we walked into a class, but I tell you, it wasn't me their eyes fixed on. Laura only had the one sibling. A much older brother. And I envied that because I had three of each.

She didn't have homemade clothes or hand-me-downs. I did. Not that I'm saying we weren't well dressed or anything like that, because we were. Our mum was a dab hand on her Singer treadle sewing machine and she made everything! She made curtains and did a lot of reupholstery. She made our dad's suits. She knitted, too, and mum had always got 'something' on the go, that she was making.

Laura's mum went out to work, and all her clothes came from the catalogue. She'd always got something new - and trendy. "Why don't you get a catalogue mum?," I said. And after a very lengthy, detailed explanation of why she would never be in debt, nor having a single thing on the 'never-never', I wished I hadn't asked, and I didn't again.

In fact, I think her thrift and handiwork talents rubbed off a little on me, so much so that I started to go to local jumble sales and buy things for their aesthetics, the different fabrics, etc. and started to make my own creations. I was actually quite proud of my efforts too, but Laura always had to take me down a peg or two and chuckle, usually within earshot of the rest of the class. But as I said, she was my best friend. And when all and sundry gazed at her, at least they must've seen me too?

You see, I was very envious of Laura. Not only because she was the prettiest girl in school, but she had £5 pocket money every week. All to herself. She bought magazines! Imagine that! I'd eventually have them, after she'd had them for a couple of weeks. She bought expensive make-up. From a department store, or chemist. NAMED brands.

My meagre make-up bag contained products from the market, or Woolies if there was any reduced. Let's face it, expensive make-up wasn't going to turn me into a raving beauty overnight, and as my delightful brother constantly reminded me "you can't make a silk purse out of a sow's ear". (I've always despised him!). So my £2 a week wages from my Saturday morning hairdressing job, had to last me!

Ha! That sounds quite fortuitous doesn't it? Saturday morning hairdressing job. I was the hair washer, sweeper up, towel washer, tea maker, general dogsbody. And I loved it. My hard earned £2 bought all my needs. Birthday and Christmas presents, jumble sale bargains, make-up, "going out"… AND supplemented my friend, time and time again. It had always been this way. "Sal, lend me a quid 'til Friday. I'll pay you back, I promise".

I don't know whether it was her angelic face and blonde hair that managed to bag her the modelling job for Christian Dior or the fact that she became very friendly with her dad's golfing partner. Ironically, coincidentally the MD of Christian Dior. Oh we all knew SHE'D go far!

And me? I opened up a little boutique of my own. Still going to jumble sales for that exquisite find. That dress that came from the 60's that I turned into a unique ball gown, or something else. It paid my rent, my holidays to Bali, and more. And yes I still bought my make-up from the market because old habits die hard.

And old habits died hard with Laura, too, because every now and again I'd get the phone call to meet up at HER favourite trendy wine bar and if I hadn't actually paid for all we drank then I'd most certainly end up having to call (and pay for!) the damn taxi to take the lush back to her very expensive elite, flat!

But the worm is turning. She's 25 now. Earns a darned sight more in a month than I do in twelve! I did notice her looks. Well, the dark circles were a dead give away! And she'd talk… incessantly. She became erratic at times, too. I wondered where my friend had gone! So I did what a best friend would do. I felt dreadful. Embarrassed at my very thinking the unthinkable. But you always know your gut instincts are usually right, don't you? And for once, my gut didn't let me down.

I parked up outside her flat one night. I knew she was there because I'd just left her there! And I waited. I waited because she'd been on the phone while I was there but she took her phone into her bedroom, so that I wouldn't hear the conversation. But she hadn't taken into account the whole bottle of champagne she'd downed and her voice was desperate.

That's when she asked me to lend her some more money. "For the last time". So when I saw the guys go to her flat, I KNEW I was right all along. And I did what I had to do, for Laura. The police arrived discretely and I saw her and the two drug dealer thugs handcuffed, being taken away by three policeman.

The headlines in the paper the next morning had me shaking like a leaf. Christian Dior's top model in such a scandal. I wonder if she'll ever get another modelling contract like that? She's now in rehab, and she's doing really really well. She's getting help, at last.

I'm at the rehab centre now, visiting her... *after all, isn't that what best friends do?*

Part Two: Things That Go Bump in the Night

We all have things that frighten us or keep us up at night. Some are vivid memories that haunt us to our dying days. Others are the wrongs, intentional or otherwise, that people have done to us along the way. Still others reflect on childhood innocence lost.

In the next section, Lisa captures a small portion of the things that certainly do "go bump in the night," both in our minds and in real life.

From ghoulies and ghosties
And long-leggedy beasties
And things that go bump in the night,
Good Lord, deliver us!

Traditional Scottish Prayer

"Fake-believe"

Do YOU believe in the afterlife? In visions, foresight, dreams?
Coincidence or destiny? Is everything life seems?

Telepathy, astrology. Horoscopes and tarot.
Crystal balls and fortune tellers. Cupid's bow and arrow.
Four-leaf clovers. Ghouls and ghosts. Hallowe'en, and UFO's.
Lucky heather. Black horse shoes. Magic lanterns. April Fools.
Angels, mermaids, unicorns. Effigies and dolls of corn.

Black cats and broomsticks. Broken mirrors. Candlesticks.
Wishing wells and shooting stars. Magic spells and silver charms.

Toss the coin, kiss the dice. Amulets, fables, Nursery Rhymes.
Fairytales and fantasies. Mistletoe to steal a kiss.

Knock-on-wood or take a chance? True love found at first-sight glance?

Magic mushrooms, healing stones, essential oils, wishing bones.
Potions. Chanting. The Evil Eye. 666, and ONE magpie.
The Holy Grail. Shangri La. 10 o'clock horses after dark.

Superstitions, myths, magicians. Old wives's tales.
Apparitions.
Mermaids, pixies, rabbits' feet. Fortune cookies, chimney sweeps.

Werewolves, vampires, monsters, dragons.
Legends, curses, spells, and demons.
A rainbow's promised pot 'o gold. 7's a secret never told.
Rumpelstiltskin, Santa Claus. Seances and Ouija Boards…
Phew! And so the list goes on!

It might be one humongous con to lure all non-believers.
perfected over centuries by legendary deceivers.
Do these myths and folklore stand, or is it all baloney?
'Fingers crossed' we will not die 'til it's proven testimony.

"Seven Deadly Sins"

I had seven cardboard boxes
and I'd labelled every one.
There's Tony, Adam, George and Rick,
Ivan, Doug, and John.

Seven cardboard boxes,
all stored beneath my bed.
Each contains a dirty deed
of something best kept dead.

Filled with wicked evil lies
and secrets never spoken.
Emblazoned with a blood red heart,
bleeding, sad, and broken.

So do I now reveal your guilt
and lay your dark souls bare?
Perhaps you've all forgotten
or indeed you may not care.

But of course you will remember.
The haunting never ends.
And time alone will never heal
or ever make amends.

So I opened up the first one,
the third one, then the last.
I laughed out loud cos I'm the one
who knows your sordid past.

I released the contents slowly
to set your conscience free.
Then I burnt those seven boxes.
Your secrets' safe with me.

Hallowe'en revenge

Every year the youths around here
torment our neighbourhood!
The thrills and joys of Hallowe'en
to them's misunderstood.

Witches, demons, ghouls and ghosts,
all masks they hide behind.
Demanding booze and cash or drugs.
Submit, or woe-be-tide.

The kiddies though, enjoy it.
For them - the night's pure fun.
But the teens are REALLY frightening . .
so I bought a plastic gun!

The missus wasn't happy
cos she loves the Hallowe'en:
she's a REAL 'namby-pamby'
every year she sets the scene.

She carves pumpkins, and puts lights in,
(But THIS year I'll do tricks!)
Makes the whole house look enticing,
(The TREAT's all mine . . . you dicks.)

Talk of 'malice with aforethought'!
Let me say what else I bought.
A ruddy huge plucked cockerel.
And not the frozen sort!

The children came a'flocking,
and those kids left full of glee.
Our front door ne'er stopped knocking . .
now the scum's left all to me.

I drool with exhilaration
when I hear that 'tap tap tap'
Revenge is just a breath away . .
Walk into my trap.

I'm stood in just my boxers.
Tesco's cockerel on my hand.
My plastic gun's aimed ready
for these older kids' demand.

"Ahh!! Hello boys. Welcome, welcome.
I heard your eager knock.
Grab hold of this here weapon
and feel my fresh plucked cock.

Boy, I wish the wife had filmed it!
They stood there, petrified!
Tears ran down my inside leg,
my joy I could not hide.

Forgive my non-compassion.
and forgive my foolish game.
Perhaps they've learnt their lesson now
and won't be back again.

"Promises broken"

I saw you in the shadows . . . today.
I called to you, pleaded too, and begged you to go away.

I looked around each corner. Bolted every door.
Believe me I've tried hiding - but I can't do it any more.

You come to me in dreams at night. You're happy, free, and calm.
Evidently dying hasn't done you any harm.

But I did, I really saw you. And felt you brush right by.
I sensed you and I smelt you, and I know you're here and why?

The candle flickers on the sill, 'tis yet another sign.
Reminding me of a deed too bad I deserve to serve some 'time'.

Secrets, lies, and promises. I buried them with you.
Now time is gnawing at my soul and karma's overdue.

I can't escape your clutches. You'll find me that's for sure.
I've tried to say I'm sorry, it's what I've been praying for.

I was hungry. REALLY hungry. And I loved chicken fricassee.
An' though I promised I'd never eat yer . . I did so, anyway!

"Suffer the little children…"

Patrick now is 65 he's lots of time to think.
Sixty-something years ago; gone within a blink.

Haunted ever by his past: it's always been that way.
He camouflaged his sordid years by lying, every day.

Inventing happy memories. A family, kids, a wife.
Eluding all such horrors that still traumatise his life.

Ireland in the 40's. Children's homes, all full.
Men of cloth protecting? A load of 'cock and bull'.

Five years old it started. Frightened, scared, and maimed.
A sweet young boy (and just a child) . . . his innocence was claimed.

Like many in that children's home (indeed they took their share!),
Patrick washed the blood and filth, from ragged underwear.

16 next and off he's packed to seek a life anew.
His past is his to keep and he will ne'er again speak true.

54
© 2020 Lisa Talbott

The years rolled into decades as he yearned for love at last
Rejecting every stretched out hand, reminders of his past.

He'd tried to leave it all behind, he'd tried to act so brave,
but knowing Patrick, as I do, he'll take this to his grave.

"The night before Christmas"

I'd hung my stocking by the fire, early Christmas Eve;
but mum n dad had friends round who I hypnotised to
leave!

I was far far too excited to stay up with all their mates.
I'm eight years old. I want my bed. It's getting very late!

Mum n dad were drinking; you could tell they'd had a lot
cos mum fell on the Christmas tree! Totally lost the plot.

It was midnight when the friends left so was down to me of
course
to get carrots for the reindeer; mince pies for Santa Claus.

I also got some Brandy cos it's Santa's favourite drink.
I'd written too a 'thank-you' note: all left by the sink.

Mum n dad went off to bed, the house left in its mess.
What the heck, tomorrow morn will be much worse I guess.

Well I didn't really sleep good 'cos I tried to stay awake.
Hoping I could get a glimpse of Santa in his wake.

And then I heard some movement! I froze: I dared not
breathe.
Santa Claus was in my house, here - cos I believe.

He was very very noisy though; perhaps he's like my dad, too much brandy whilst on route which went right to his head?

But my childhood dreams were shattered. No magic there to see.
No Christmas gifts, no Barbie bike, just a broken Christmas tree!

My parents, in their fuddled state, dialled 999.
Christmas had been stolen and I cried and cried and cried.

Why would Santa do this? He's meant to give, not steal!
I don't like him any more, and I don't think he's real.

He even stole our turkey so we had sausages instead.
Santa Claus I hate you and I wish that you were dead!

(From Meggie Tyler, eight years old. Don't forget my name!
Who'd been a good girl all year long. You can't say the same.)

"Unfriended"

You didn't like my comment. Don't you think I give a
damn?
We share a different vision because this is who I am.

Is friendship really measured by my views, or by your
needs?
I loved you for your actions, your support and your good
deeds.

Our many treasured memories lay shattered in my mind.
And I can't un-see the venom that you haven't tried to hide.

To me there was a comfort in a friendship, such as ours.
Chaff and grain together, we'd discuss it all, for hours.

If I was right and you were wrong, or the other way around,
it mattered not a fraction, we would both be safe an' sound.

But it took one little posting, to which you disagreed.
Hence your anger's turned on me and I am shocked indeed!

Let us talk it about it properly; over coffee like we do.
We can put it all behind us, don't give up on me and you.

I don't like spaghetti: you adore the stuff on toast.
You like fish on Sunday whereas I prefer a roast!

I love gin and tonic, yours is always rum and coke.
You've the perfect husband - I don't even have a bloke.

We should agree to disagree, it's what we're both about.
Well, it's how it always used to be before this 'cyber'
shout.

Your messages were cruel and sharp and hurt me to the
core.
I'd never heard you air the views you've written here,
before!

I wish you'd told me privately, not there for all to see.
And now the world's aware of what you truly think of me.

20 years of friendship; now so fractious it can't mend.
Then you logged on to my profile, and sadly pressed
'unfriend'.

A boy called Mark"

There's a boy they can't find, in the village
and everyone's going berserk.
I like the boy Mark, who's gone missing,
though at school, they call him a jerk.

See, the boy who's gone missing's 11.
But he's clever. Cunning. Astute.
His mum and his grandma adore him.
And he's got the whole town in pursuit.

It was mum who had searched the house over.
It was she who was straight on the phone.
She screamed to deaf walls in her hallway:
bereft, he'd been left 'home alone'.

The police cars arrived within minutes.
Well aware, of Mark's 'special needs'.
They'd brought dogs; (Alsatians and Shepherds).
I love dogs. Love ALL doggy breeds.

The radio begged reinforcements,
as 'copter blades roared overhead.
The TV showed Mark smiling sweetly,
and neighbours cried, fearing him dead.

(But I'm NOT dead. I'm here in the attic.
And I'm tired, and bored now it's dark.
So I'd better come out now from hiding.
It's been fun being 'missing boy Mark')

"A web of deceit"

Oh what a tangled web we weave
to lure and trap, and then deceive
the innocents and sweet naive,
on silken threads of make-believe.

We're liars, fools; we flout the rules;
we taunt and haunt, like ghosts and ghouls.
Use words and deeds and ridicules
inflicting pain, like battle tools.

We cheat and hurt, we dish the dirt.
We're constantly on Red Alert
to skim the truth, and then avert
our eyes to those we disconcert.

So stop this spin; we can but try.
Let's cross our hearts and hope to die
to never leave folk high an' dry.
T'is time to blind one's evil eye.

"Dorian"
A Short Story

Leigh wasn't fully asleep. She was at that stage where, give another five minutes, and he'd see her REM and he could relax a little. But still he watched her, wondering for the millionth time what sleep actually felt like. He'd never slept. Wasn't any need. Dorian had been given a new assignment; his last one was over and it had pained him immensely. It was also his longest assignment.

He'd never questioned his boss's orders, ever. It hadn't occurred to him that there would've been an option not to. He enjoyed his work. Or actually, did he? Again, he didn't question it. Assignments were assignments and what the boss said, he did! Like they all did. So now Leigh was in a deep slumber and this afforded Dorian an opportunity to reminisce.

He reminisced over his many assignments but the last one was still quite prevalent in his thoughts and he felt a strange and overwhelming feeling of sadness. Now that was a first! A unique experience for him. How odd! Actually, no. It wasn't the first experience. It was the second. He shrugged, nonchalantly, dismissing the urge to check his pulse, and remind himself that he was without emotion. He tried to recall his colleagues' conversations as to whether or not any of them had ever become 'emotionally attached'? He couldn't. They didn't. But the sadness enveloped him as he watched Leigh sleep. In Leigh, he saw Evelyn. Eve, as she was known to by everyone. *HIS* Eve!

"Mum!!! Come and watch me climb this tree". She was a six year old nightmare! It was a complete surprise to her parents that their daughter had managed to celebrate her 6th birthday. Disregarding the fact Evelyn had been born two months prematurely, and she was a 'blue baby', she miraculously defied all odds and was a constant bewilderment to all and sundry that she was as normal as one could ever describe Eve as being.

Liz flew to the tree where she saw her daughter precariously dangling by her legs that were wrapped around a branch of a fig tree that was right outside the kitchen portico. How many times had she nagged Luke to chop that ruddy tree down, she'd no idea! And there's the apple of his eye hanging upside down like a bat. Her life fair flashed before her! And that was Dorian's first introduction to this beautiful, blonde, blue-eyed, angelic... nightmare! He was going to have his work cut out. Oh boy!

Frankie stirred on Leigh's bed. The cheeky monkey shouldn't be on the damn bed! His little white paws tapped gently at her face, reminding her to feed him again for the tenth time that day. She threw back her duvet, still with her eyes closed, picked up the feline interruption, and left him outside her bedroom door. Dorian held his breath, though there was no need. And then back to land of the nod.

"Why am I feeling I've walked this path before?" Thought Dorian. He'd heard of the expression *"Deja-vu"* but hadn't FELT it. Ever. All of Dorian's assignments had been different. Some lasted longer than others, too. It wasn't in the 'rules' to question or think about anything. He and his colleagues were all there to carry out a 'role'.

Eve was indeed precarious. Dorian wondered why she'd been born a girl! she was definitely as crazy as any adolescent youth! He'd been by her side throughout her wild childhood, steering her towards finding her Mr Right as a young woman. He watched her blossom as a mother. A grandmother. And he'd been there at her side, comforting her whilst she mourned the passing of her beloved soul mate. It was his job. His assignment. And when Eve graciously took her last breath on Earth, Dorian was there, as he'd ever been, watching over her. 'Protecting' her.

Another team arrived to collect Eve and take her over to her new destination. It had been a wonderful assignment. He'd enjoyed every moment of the 80 years. What a privilege. And Leigh was his new assignment. Leigh was going to be, unbeknown to her, protected.

"Hello Leigh, I'm Dorian. You don't know me. You'll never know me. The boss tells me you're a crazy girl so he's sent me to look out for you. You're gonna sell that motorbike girl, I can tell you now. You see, I'm your Guardian Angel. You can call me Dorian."

The REM in Leigh's eyes stop abruptly! Bolt upright she sits in her bed. "Dorian . . ?" "Wow, what a dream that was! Frankie? Frankie are you there? Come here, come sleep on my bed. I'll look after you"

Part Three: In Sickness and in Health

Illness affects all of us. It is a certainty. We can't run from it. We can't hide from it. We can only accept it and get on with our lives.

However, the poignancy of Lisa's poetry, particularly about serious medical conditions, should strike a chord with anyone who has dealt with severe illness. One of the works in this section, "Take my hand," touched me very deeply. My wife, Sandy, and I lost our eldest son, Adam, to cancer ten years before this book was written. Thanks to Lisa's work, I can envision his journey to "the other side" being guided by my own father, who had passed away 24 years earlier – and then Adam welcoming his other grandfather (Sandy's dad) through the Pearly Gates just a couple of years later. We hope that Adam will be waiting there for us well!

I urge you to have a box of tissues handy as you read this next section. Tears of sadness and laughter are likely!

"My boob job"

There're several words one dreads to hear.
And 'Cancer' fills us all with fear.
It raced, my pulse. My heart went 'thump'
. . .the day I found a little lump.

I tried not dwelling much at first.
I picked an' prodded: never hurt.
(See, pimple popping's just my thing;
I love to delve and dig right in.)

Did nothing short of gouging out,
but couldn't eke the poison out.
'Twas then the doc confirmed to me
my boobs contained the dreaded C.

Not one but two, both had to go;
and I've a 'train-line' wound to show.
I tell you now, it's bloody strife
these tell-tell signs of a surgeon's knife.

Chemo next for several months
ensuring I don't get more bumps.
I lost my hair. I lost three stones.
Was nothing but a bag o'bones.

Lace front wigs and padded bras
camouflage depressive scars.
My eyes are black, my face is grey
but hey, I live and breathe today.

But last not least of this disdain?
I won't have droopy boobs again.
In fact I personally, here attest,
I LOVE my newly sculptured chest.

*I'm dedicating this poem to all you amazing ladies
everywhere who are battling - or who have beaten - breast
cancer, and especially to Kylee Cameron, niece of Sandy
and Mike Hurd, who is currently enduring her own battle
with breast cancer. //LT*

"Dear Santa"

Dearest Santa, let me say
I've loved you since forever-a-day.
Grew up with you; as all kids do.
And every year I've thought of you.

You brought us toys and countless joys.
(Indeed for all the girls and boys.)
You cast your magic every year
creating memories; cherished dear.

Oh Santa dear. Remember me?
back in 1953?
I was ten, in a hospice bed.
I had a tumour in my head.

You ho ho ho'd. You beamed your smile.
We sat and chatted quite a while.
I held your hand, in trepidation
as you described my operation.

70

You left, and I tried hard to sleep.
I wanted this whole night to keep.
And you made my Christmas wish come true.
I'm better now, thanks to you!

Since that Christmas - years long gone,
(66 if I'm not wrong)
I tried to glimpse you every time
to thank you for this life of mine.

We never met again of course,
My cancer left with no recourse.
I left that hospice six months after
in the echo of your laughter.

Dearest Santa. My old saviour.
Grant this old girl one last favour.
(I'm much too old to hang a stocking
and Lord above my memory's shocking)
Tell me truly did I see, that Christmas Eve of '53
You, and matron, in the snow . . .
Kissing 'neath the mistletoe?

Man flu

Christmas now's all over.
I blinked - and it was gone.
I'm feeling pretty awful: I don't think I'll be 'here' long!

I'm wrapped up in my duvet
and I've hankies by the score.
I've blown my nose a thousand times and now it's really
sore.

I'm coughing, sneezing, snotty.
My throat, it hurts like hell.
My temperature's through the ceiling and I really don't feel
well.

My wife's not sympathetic,
she just doesn't understand.
(I swear sometimes that woman lives away in la la land!)

But my symptoms quickly worsened,
I was 'throwing up' all day.
My stomach cramped in agony and the loo's too far away!!

I felt a sneeze approaching.

Released it with such force

and ashamed beyond belief because I 'followed through' of

course!

Red faced and sobbing loudly.

Not a soul to heed my shouts.

My bedding's full of vomit . . and last night's Brussels

sprouts!

Oh the smell, the shock, the horror!

Not least - embarrassment.

And I prayed the Lord would spare me . . dying in my

excrement.

Take my hand

The bed felt safe, yet all too stark.

The screen, the lightness in the dark.

The nurses' chatter tells him life goes on around, outside.

Why does sleep evade him? Even though he's oh so tired.

He didn't have a party and he didn't have a cake.

He'd have one when he's home again, and if he stays awake.

He'll have the bike he wanted; and that trip to Disneyland but he needs to speak to grandad first and make him understand.

This man, he's never met before, yet sits beside his bed,

knows so much about him yet no words were ever said.

A kindly man, looks like his dad, and his Uncle Ben.

And he wished he could go home to play with all his friends again.

He hasn't been to school for months, this illness is a killer.
He hasn't left his bed and tears saturate his pillow.
His grandad never leaves him; he just sits there in a chair.
He thinks it's strange his mum and dad don't talk to grandad, there.

Transfusions now are weekly, and he trusts his nice young nurse.
But can't unhear his mother's words "cancer is a curse".
He feels he ought to tell the man to leave: to go away.
He isn't ready for their trip, he's better every day.

But better he's not getting and the screen beeps one last cry.
He didn't get to see his mum or dad to say goodbye.
He hopes they'll both forgive him and one day will understand.
Until that time, he takes his wings . . . and his grandad's hand.

(For Adam…)

"Peeling back the layers".

See this wound? It will not mend.
'Normal' folk won't comprehend.
I act so false, keep plugging on;
tortured in my world, gone wrong.
I laugh, I joke,
yet no-one hears my stifled choke.
I wear a painted smile each day
and pray my black dog goes away.
No-one reads between my lies
and see the ME not my disguise.
I act so well, I fool you all.
I lack no guile nor wherewithal.
I tried to peel away each layer,
but not traversing anywhere.
Do not feel shame,
you're not to blame,
I'm the one 'hands up' to say,
I'm sorry I behave this way.
So hear my screams and watch me bleed,
patience from you's all I need.
The tunnel's dark, tho strange, feels right.
I run euphoric into light.
When will I be free of pain?
Help me! Help me mend again.

"Taking stock, or stock taking?"

A cheeky damn policeman pulled me over yesterday.
I'm breaking rules, the guy declared: get back home and stay!

I'd only bought essentials just to last a week or two.
Everybody needs supplies so what else could I do?

I travelled in my car alone, playing by the rules.
Masked up to the eyeballs, keeping distance from the fools.

I raced my Lidl trolley to the aisle that had the gin
and then considered mother so I put some white wine in.

I'm not a fan of beer but it's best to not run low,
(just in case some friends drop by, cos hey - you never know.)

So I got my lot, I paid by card, and loaded up my booty.
Driving back (and weighted down!) was pulled by 'Mr Snooty'.

Take a look yourself" I said, "these are MY essentials!"
I gotta get my fix t'night, so shove yer damn Credentials.

A happy chappy he was not and tried to write a fine!
Reluctantly the bribe had cost me mother's box of wine.

Sixteen gins and tonics. Vodkas? I got ten.
Brandy, whisky, rum and coke, a six pack - for the men.

'Cos when all of this is over and we're fine, alive and hearty,
I've a garage full of everything. Welcome to my party!

"Reflections"
A Short Story

Ah, there goes young Anthony on his way to school again this morning. Such a happy little chappie he is. A bit of a character too by the looks of those plasters on his knee and his scraped shoes. Well, not 'proper' shoes as I'd call them. Trainers, I think they're called. Ha ha, trainers for shoes indeed. In my day, 'trainers' were worn on a different part of the anatomy, and it wasn't on the feet! My oh my. Now see, MY Brian didn't need trainers for too long. Oh, he was as bright as a button. Walking at 12 months and in 'big boy' pants soon after. I was lucky with Brian. The poly-opposite of his dear dad.

His dad… Let me tell you… Oh where to begin? Clifford had been on the trawlers. He told of fascinating tales at sea. It wasn't what he wanted to do; he knew he was going to get his call-up papers and thought he'd avoid it by travelling to Liverpool to get a job on the trawlers. It wasn't long though before he realised there was no escaping his duty. Frank was there at the docks that Sunday evening when they'd returned from a fishing trip, waiting with Cliff's papers. He never did lose that 'ten to two' lilt. It made me chuckle. I found it quite endearing.

No, Brian was nothing like his dad. He was more into sports. Football mad he was. Always dreamt of becoming a professional footballer. I suppose young Anthony's the same and that's why he's got plasters over his knees. And I expect his mum tells him the same as we'd tell Brian "there's no money to be made playing football"!

Well I never! There's Lucy just walked by! I haven't seen that young woman in a while. Don't know how the brazen madam dare show her face 'round these parts after all THAT scandal. Oh you didn't hear? "Juicy Lucy" they called her. God rest her poor mother. She must've been wracked with shame. I'm sure she had ideas on my Brian at one stage but, like I say, he was as bright as a button. Set his sights higher than a little trollop like her, thank the Lord. Their family took in lodgers. Many fairground folk when the fairs came to the village. I've no doubt that 'Juicy Lucy' offered a tad more on the tariff than just B&B. But that's just gossip, I'm sure.

I'm waiting for my sister whilst I sit here. I've been meaning to write to her for a while but my hand's giving me some 'gyp' so I'm relying on telepathy. Haha. No, not really, I'm jesting. she usually pops round on a Friday. Is it Friday today? It must be because it was Thursday yesterday. Top-of-the-Pops was on and Cliff recorded it. He always records it so we can listen to the top ten in the week and woe betide anyone who makes a noise while he tapes it. I think he has a bit of a crush on one of those Pans People dancers, Babs, that one with the long blonde hair. Didn't she get married to Peter Powell, you know - that good looking chap who played Jesus?

The fellas are still there, outside, sawing that monstrosity of a tree down. About time too, if you ask me. It's a danger, I tell you. Wouldn't surprise me in the least if young Anthony deemed to climb it one day and did himself a mischief. S'been there for such a long long time, but everything these days has a "sell-by" date. And that's another nonsense. We didn't have "sell-by" dates on the bread we bought from our baker. Nor on the potatoes from the market. What is the world coming to? I'll be glad when that racket they're making, is over and I can enjoy a bit of peace and quiet again. There's no respect any more.

I'm glad my Brian isn't disrespectful. I'm sure he would appreciate the fact that his dad and I hid that letter from the football association inviting him to trial for the county football team when he was a teenager. He wouldn't have had that good job in the factory, that's for sure. Well. I can't sit here all day dilly dallying. I'd best get a move on.

Get my silly self dressed and bake a cake for when my sister arrives. "Have a lovely day at school Anthony". Bless him.

"Good morning Vera, and how are you this lovely morning?"... "Vera, are you awake love?" "Let's get you up and dressed. June's doing her rounds with the tea trolley, and she'll be here in a tick. Vera . . . VERA! . . . oh Vera".

Part Four: Try to Keep Your Dignity

Life just isn't fair. We get poked and prodded in bodily orifices when we visit our health care providers. Certain tests take away our dignity, revealing parts of our bodies that rarely (if ever) see the light of day.

Outside of the doctor's office, our own clumsiness gets in the way. We fall... we have other accidents... and when people find out about them, we all want to tell the best story possible, even if it stretches the truth "a wee bit."

Other times, we (or our families) do things that embarrass us. We can't hide those things, but we certainly can do our best to smile and carry on. Maybe even have a good laugh!

Once again, Lisa's ability to highlight the essence of life's little indignities in verse shines through. Some of them had me in paroxysms of laughter. Others, well... just read and make your own decision!

"Mansplaining humility"

I had to go to hospital on Monday, 9 o'clock.
I tell you, I was nervous so arrived there on the dot.

I won't be too descriptive but I'll give you several clues.
I had to take to hospital a sample of my stools.

It's really quite revolting to discuss one's toilet ways
but I hadn't 'been' for ages; in fact for several days.

When I did so, oh the agony whilst sitting on the throne.
No sympathy from 'her in doors', all 'fat lass' does is
moan.

It's ruddy darned uncomfortable when sitting for a while
and a grimace has replaced my usual enigmatic smile.

So hence this little visit - to find out what's amiss.
"The doctor for all arseholes" bade my dearest with a kiss.

There on doctor's table I'm positioned on all fours.
If I should see that doc again, I pray it's 'after doors'.

'cos I will grab him by his neck and land him one humdinger.
Was there really any need to do what he did with his finger?

"A simple case of piles" he said, and tossed his gloves aside.
(I do not know which hurt the most, the finger or my pride!)

I leapt from off that table grabbed my 'sample' from his desk.
How can people do this job? It really is grotesque.

I came home pretty sullen, to the wife's sarcastic jokes.
Emasculated, soul deflated. Heaven help us blokes.

"My mammogram"

My mammogram test was pending (such things us ladies dread).
But we're thankful for these tests they do . . rather that than dead.

I had to prep beforehand, (i.e. I shaved my pits),
and sorted out a new lace bra to boost my sagging bits.

I told my boss that morning that I needed time off work.
"They need photos of my boobs sir" (and how my boss did smirk).

"We could do all that for you. We'll take some pics today".
(I think that very statement was a hefty cheque away!)

So, I parked up in the car park; fed the meter several quid.
Sniffed below my shoulders ' case of B.O. - god forbid.

The left boob first, and then the right.
Pressed it flat, and squeezed it tight!
Turn your face, an' lift your chin.
The pain and stress of my chagrin!

The indignation suffered is dismissed by all our men.
They'd cringe and flail, an' all turn tail, if the same was done to them.

My results were satisfactory.
There was nothing in my midst.
Which goes to prove that even now . . .
I still have perfect tits!

"Bear false witness"

Ooh; the house next door was vandalised. Shock horror on
their faces!
They'd just got back from Tenerife. Not even unpacked
cases.

Broken glass lay all about; their window truly smashed.
Imagine coming home to find your sanctuary's been
trashed.

Well me, the perfect neighbour, called the cops and made a
brew.
Patronised and sympathised and "anything I can do?"

I told the burly handsome cop I hadn't seen a thing.
(Partly true, I didn't have my contact lenses in).

But really I'm a liar; my excuse was far too lame.
It started off an accident; my dog's the one to blame.

Playing ball I threw it monumentally askew.
Broke their window; dog ran off, and I, indeed, did too.

My street now think we're targets for all vandals near and
wide.
So I'm bolting MY back door as well . . and keep the dog
inside!

© 2020 Lisa Talbott

"The flora thief"

The house next door is empty. A ruin, truth be told.
It's actually for sale right now and worth it's weight in
gold.

Miles and miles of woodland. The most amazing view.
Next door is worth a fortune; if you've a hundred grand or
two.

Been empty now for decades. Hence it's in a state.
But the fruit trees and the flowers there! Such a wicked
waste.

Apples, lemons, cherries. Roses 'round the door.
Wisteria climbing up the walls . . . .
. . . and what I went there for!

I donned my boots and gard'ning gloves. Secateurs in hand;
braved the nettles - weeds an' all, to rob this 'No man's
Land'.

Such a gorgeous bounty. Could not believe my luck.
A mass of colour, sights an' smells . .
but then my foot got stuck!

See, the foxes and the wildlife - have also laid a claim:
raising young ones, 'neath the ground, I screamed and
writhed in pain!

No-one knew my trauma, cos no-one heard me yell.
No one knew I was there or why . .
yet I screamed like bloody hell!

Two days, stuck in that fox hole. Just imagine that!
No loo roll, toothpaste, food or wine . . stunk like a damn
polecat!

Now all clad in plaster cast; ten more weeks like this!
I'm being spoilt, waited on. Life is bloomin' bliss!

"Why I had a career change"

Are your work pals mad and crazy and invite you out to
play?
You procrastinate, as usual, but you'll be there anyway.

You declare "won't be a late one" and insist "just one or
two".
You've to be at work tomorrow and hungover will not do.

'course those plans fly out the window with the first Dom
Pérignon
but at 15 notes a glassful no-one plans on staying long.

But our Champagne Bar's a'buzzing, and the talent's pretty
cute.
Testosterone in abundance. So to hell with resolute.

That bar draws so much 'profile' in, and hey it's such a
treat
just to mingle with the famous folk, the rich, and the elite.

Now £80's much lighter and I'm dancing like a loon
and I can't locate my colleagues though I've searched in
every room.

So I called my trusted Uber cos by now I yearn my bed
and t'was then that I remembered what my absent
colleagues said.

Our boss was at our champagne bar, with clients from The
States
whom I deemed to flaunt my assets round a pole, upon the
stage.

Cajoled them of their dollars which they tucked inside my
bra.
I taunted and convinced them I'm some famous dancing
star.

But I won't be office bound no more; in fact I daren't
return.
So I plan to man a lap dance club, cos I've dollars now to
burn.

"The Wishing Well"

Late July in '99, the sun was such a scorcher.
I'd burnt my nose, my back, my boobs. That summer felt
like torture!

But gardening chores are ever there, with weeds a'taking
over!
Buttercups and daisies and the dreaded spreading clover!

I started digging quite a hole, to make a Wishing Well.
(I'd seen one in a magazine and wanted one, as well.)

So far so good, I'm down four foot, and almost quite as
wide.
The fork got stuck, the ground fair shook, and nearly bent
the tine.

The sound of metal seemed quite odd vibrating from the
earth.
So got the trowel, to dig around; create a wider berth.

A huge great sphere, I made appear, and did so with aplomb.
Would you 'Christmas Eve' it folk, it looked quite like a bomb.

Now ladies, gents, dear readers too, I'd really not a clue.
So got a hammer from the shed to give a whack or two.

Perhaps it's just an old tin bath, buried yonks ago?
(My grandad welded skis on ours - brilliant in the snow!)

Might even be a motorbike? A treasure chest with gold?
I need to get it out damn quick, a fortune's in this hold!

And then it started ticking loud, so neither chest nor tomb.
Just some old clock, and working too! Tick tick tick tick
. . . . . BOOOOOOM!

"Banged up?"

I wish I was in Wormwood: a convict, doing 'bird'.
Life is such a doddle being 'banged up'; so I've heard.

Everything gets paid for. The 'lecky and the gas.
Three square meals each day on tap: (no alcohol, alas).

I think you might get ciggies too, perhaps some weed and
'dust'.
(Depends of course the cost of bribes and who the screws
to trust.)

Full TV and internet - no licence fee to pay
In fact you live in luxury, every single day.

No appointments for a doctor. Free too, yer pearly whites!
Heaven forbid the law pooh-poohs your basic human
rights!

No Monday morning washdays. No chores at all. How
great!
A pampered lifestyle evermore: Tell me, what's the wait?

So murder if you have to. Commit a crime or two.
Worry not the "system's" gonna well provide for you.

They'll even fix your funeral, should you cop it whilst
inside.
And the media will embellish all your virtues, near and
wide.

So if y'think that things are tough and that y'life's not
worth a dime,
perhaps you should consider now's the time to plot your
crime!

Notes from a worried mum"

Jessie . . somehow never managed getting home last night.
My stomach flipped in somersaults. Something isn't right.

'Course I've tried to call her but I'm getting no reply.
Trying to wrack my fuddled brain inventing reasons why.

I see no explanation. She's a good and lovely girl.
Scenarios play within my head: my life is in turmoil.

She went to this new nightclub which just opened
yesterday.
She's 20, so I have to let her go her own sweet way.

Why has she not called me? Someone's done her harm!
I'm feeling sick. I'll call the cops. I need to raise alarm.

The police were quite elusive said she'd not been 'missing'
long.
But goodness I'm mother so I know when something's
wrong.

I tried to keep my cool but I've seen far too much TV.
Mini skirts and cleavages, a disastrous recipe!

I called her best friend's mobile but her mum picked up
instead.
Told me she was still asleep, nursing her bad head.

No, she'd not seen Jessie. No, she knew no more.
And then there was this bang bang bang . . at my kitchen
door.

I love a man in uniform but not this morning, please!
My life fair flashed before me as I fell on shaky knees.

Oh you've found a young girls' body? No, please don't say
a thing.
Just tell me she's alive and well. I'll pledge you anything!

NO!! My daughter spent the night in cells! Nissed up as a
pewt!
Dancing naked through our town, her name in disrepute.

I'd felt sick with fear this morning. But now my fingers
itch.
Can't wait to get her home again. I'll KILL the brazen
bitch!

"I survived . . . the dentist"

I am not afraid, I am PETRIFIED.
I'm off to see the dentist at a quart t'five.
Cos I spent oh so many hours running over with my tongue,
it all felt wrong,
and I am wishing it was gone.
There's this big hole,
a crater space.
It's causing agony and bruising, and some swelling to my
face
I would've phoned at 8 o'clock and pleaded low on bended
knee,
If I'd have known just how damn painful this back
mandible would be;
so I will go. Put off no more.
Just rip it out now,
so it can't hurt me any more.
I should'a done it weeks ago, I shouldn't have even
questioned why
it's just the thought o'that damn needle makes me tremble,
sweat and cry.
Oh yes that's why. I thought I'd die.
But as long as I can still drink wine, I'm sure that I'll be
fine.
I've got plenty years to live and don't want gnashers like a
sieve,
so now's the time, to tow the line, hey hey.

It took all the pills I had just to calm my heart
trying desperately in vain to hold on to a fart.
You see my stomach churned with fear because the
dentist's sitting here
but I let go.
And he didn't even seem to know,
he couldn't tell.
It didn't smell.
Continued pulling, twisting, tugging and it bled like flippin'
hell
and then at last it's out and free and came out none too
easily
now all that's left for me to do is go and settle up his fee.
Then do no more.
It's what he's for.

I just don't get his awful job
keep poking into someone's gob.
but I don't care,
I left his chair,
Pain freeeeee.

"Why the NHS gets sued"

Dear ladies, (and you gentlemen), sit down while I begin.
I want to tell my story here, so you'll see why my chagrin.

I've just come out of hospital, for a routine, minor, op.
(Yes dear folk, in other words, I went to have 'the chop').

We're cracking on, me and 'er, and don't use
contraception.
Hence this op was vital to avoid a new conception!

The doctor reassured me these are simple operations.
Effective almost straight away (bar a few 'manipulations'!)

So I guess I was a bit surprised when told to count to ten.
I only got to five or six; was fast asleep by then.

Woke up in my pure white sheets and feeling sore, below.
The guys at work had lied (the gits) they said "you'll never
know".

And then the dreaded blow was dealt 'bout the 'cock-up'
they performed.
TWO guys share the damn same name, and IN the damn
same ward!

A youngster of just 15; what a bum decision!
That poor young lad, won't be a dad . . he only went for
circumcision.

And thus the missus overjoyed, fair raped me there and
then.
Six weeks later, joy oh joy: we're pregnant once again!

© 2020 Lisa Talbott

"Inside out"

From the outside, I look perfect.
The inside, not quite so.
The inside's badly broken.
But it's the outside here on show.

The decor's all an illusion.
Accessories, make-up, clothes.
Invite me to traverse with you?
Expect a door slammed closed.

I see my mirror image,
reflected in your eyes.
I laugh in satisfaction of my wonderful disguise.

I'll reel you, taunt you, beckon.
I'll lure you easily.
Make believe you stand a chance,
but NOT with the real me!

Text me, email, FaceTime.
Course, I'll fake I'm ok.
And I'll promise you forever -
we'll get together one day.

So you see this two-way mirror?
Do you feel me scream and shout?
It is not a true reflection.
You can't see me inside out.

Part Five: War Is Hell

Neither military service nor war are the sole domain of the Soldier, Sailor, Airman, or Marine. They have families, too. Families that love and care for them. Families that are uprooted and moved halfway around the world when a new posting comes along. Families that suffer through interminable deployments and other absences that the servicemember might not be able to talk about. Families that deal with the grief of losing a loved one in battle.

Many warriors never come home. They served their country and gave their lives in that service, protecting our freedoms and way of life. Unfortunately, they become another statistic, another gravestone, another memory that only their families or immediate brothers-in-arms will remember.

Others come home and never really leave the battlefield. What was once known as "shell shock" or "combat fatigue" is now called "Post-Traumatic Stress Disorder. The devastation these combat-related afflictions cause is incalculable and the tentacles far-reaching.

Outside of warriors and their immediate families, there is always other "collateral damage" (intentional or otherwise) involving noncombatant civilians. Jews in Nazi-occupied Europe during World War II. Japanese-Americans in internment camps in the United States. Hiroshima and Nagasaki. Kurds in northern Iraq. The list could go on and on.

Once again, Lisa has skillfully described the essence of being connected with military life or armed conflict, both directly and indirectly, sometimes going back as far as World War I. As a veteran and avowed history buff, I salute her for the vivid images she creates in this section. I have, with her permission, already shared several of the poems with military colleagues and military support organizations like the American USO.

At the end of the section, you will also find another of Lisa's masterpieces: a short story, "Haunted." It is a compelling read that portrays the emotional turmoil that one soldier faced following his time "in the trenches" of World War I.

"Our Last Dance"

I danced with you, romanced with you.
We flirted, laughed, and more.
I promised you, and prayed for you
when you went off to war.

Indeed, I prayed for all our boys
to come home safe, unharmed.
Your letters were the only joy
that kept me sane and calm.

Camaraderie too, I envied you,
friendships in all forms.
Though parted in those killing fields
by foreign uniforms.

Summers turned to autumn.
Winters, then the spring.
Years rolled by unmercifully
in a world that wreaked of sin.

But you did come home - in body.
That, and a broken mind.
You couldn't sleep and you didn't talk;
your soul was left behind.

Our dance was never stepped the same
as sunshine turned to grey.
Our love was killed in No Mans' Land,
and left there . . to decay.

"My turn"

Welcome home big brother, you've been gone for far too
long.
Brother how we're saddened. Glad you're back where you
belong.

Our mum read all your letters out, (well, those she did
receive).
The last that she received from you was of 'that Christmas
Eve'.

Did you really play with Jerries? Downed arms to join the
crowd?
Played footie, joked, and laughed that day? Oh brother, I'm
so proud!

(I too have just enlisted so could fight there by your side
and was just about to join you when that telegram arrived.)

Remember your mate Freddie and his stallion, Proud
Command?
Did you know they went there too, and died in No-Man's
Land?

Freddie too is coming home - him, but not his horse.
And mother's getting anxious that I'm leaving soon, of
course.

We heard you'd been found cradled in some foreign rugged
arms:
a tear stained wounded Jerry, with Mum's photo in his
palms.

The buntings all prepared and we've a bugler here as well.
The Last Post's played to honour you boys back from
bloody Hell.

Family, friends, and neighbours gather here for you and
Fred.
You've done your due, your battle's done, it's my turn now
instead.

"The wedding dress"

When I was just a young girl,
I had such vivid dreams.
I longed to be a Goddess
with my name on silver screens.

I'd imagine I was famous,
Like Liz Taylor, or Bardot,
and made my sisters act with me
(a bossy so and so).

Even through my teen years
my head was in the clouds
I loved the hype and glamour
of a world so out-of-bounds.

And still I yearned the status
of the high society
yet couldn't live the dream I sought
of notoriety.

Then just as I had given up,
Prince Charming came along.
I pictured wedded bliss and kids
and make our own swan song.

But fate held other plans for me
and for my Prince Charming too.
My love was taken in the war
and he, just twenty-two.

My wedding dress still hangs there;
fragile now, with age.
I never got to wear that dress,
my life was more 'backstage'.

But I'll wear my dress this nighttime.
I'm 90 now, you see.
And I'll dance with my Prince Charming,
who'll be here tonight, for me.

"I was a Land Girl"

I used to live in Civvy Street, just before the war.
I'd never spent a single night away from home before.

But women too had duties so to farmlands I was bound.
Cotton sheets n'feather beds all luxuries left behind.

I caught the train to Norfolk to this massive dairy farm.
The setting 'picture perfect' though our quarters held no charm.

I'd never seen a cow before, nor sheep nor pigs, or hens
And here I learned to milk 'em, feed 'em: cleaning out their pens.

We rise an' shine 5.30 for our dripping, bread, and tea.
But slipping into 'farming life' was no mean feat for me.

There were six of us together. Girls from near and far.
Eager yearning Friday nights for sing songs at the bar!

We had 'Eyeties' too, and Germans. Mario, Fritz, José.
Far too much testosterone for Land Girls of that day.

Mario worked with metals. He was clever with his hands!
He worked a ring from sixpence (a kind of engagement
band).

I had to leave the farm because my friends I couldn't face.
Three months 'gone' at nineteen years, I'd fallen, sinned,
disgraced.

I named my girl Maria, in memory of your name.
She wears that sixpence ring you gave me, on a silver
chain.

I never left you Mario. Even though I'm 95.
My grandson, he's your namesake, and he keeps our love
alive.

*Dedicated to my lovely friend, Jean, who never found out
what happened to her beloved Mario, and whose ring she
always wore round her neck. Through the magic of social
media, I was able to locate Jean in 2020, now 95 and in a
nursing home, and share this poem with her through her
daughter. //LT*

"In black and white"

The sheer delight to reminisce.
To feel the the past, relive the bliss.
To flick through albums, smeared with dust,
and feel again forgotten lust.

To see myself as I looked that day,
exclaiming loudly, in dismay
"I can't believe I wore that dress,
and goodness grief, my hair's a mess"

But camera's then couldn't cheat or lie;
all laid bare to the viewers eye.
Immortalised in black and white . .
The day I wed my Mr Right.

Oh so many moons ago.
Why did it all go wrong?
Someone turn the clocks back please
I yearn my old swan song.

But the photographs, whilst silent,
mock me . . lying here.

Visions now all faded,
fragments of yesteryear.

1940 April 1st. No humour to impart.
A telegram, with words on . .
so few to break a heart

Now I'll pack away this album,
It's best left in the past.
I'll store it in the attic,
with the rest of junk amassed.

"I love/d you, Dad"

I'm hiding in the pantry, tight against the wall.
Next to all the ham and eggs, stacked up on the thrall.

I'm hiding from my daddy (please don't come inside!)
I know he's had a 'skin full' and he'll want to tan some
hide.

My dad is really lovely; well he was before the war.

Played with us, an' laughed a lot, but that was all before…

And oh extremely handsome: I said I'd marry him.
I wouldn't now; my dad has changed, he's now a scary
thing!

I've a sister and a brother and our mum is just the best.
And life at home was brilliant, 'til dad came home, a mess.

Our mother's doing washing for the neighbours in our
street.
"It's only for a while" she says, 'til dad's back on his feet.

Dad's feet are really fine though, it's mum who's in denial.
They get him to the pub each night . . and still pull rank and
file.

We hear him in the nighttime. His screams, my mothers
too!
Cos mother bears the scars of war like she had been there
too.

I think it's really late now. Mum's asleep upstairs.
His dinner's on the gas stove (and he says that no one
cares!).

But we do! We did! Oh daddy! I'm trembling with fear.
Don't come in the pantry please. Pretend that I'm not here.

"The Violinist of Auschwitz"

The soldiers pounded wintery streets with orders from the Reich.
Neighbours, families, friends and foe, vanished; day and night.

Herded into cattle trucks. Vermin's what we are.
Persecuted. Extradited. Forced to wear the star.

Bewildered children at a loss to what was going on.
Frantic families clung together, steadfast in their throng.

Hundreds to every carriage. No water, food, nor care.
The stench of vomit, shit, and piss permeate the air.

The snow shone bright on Auschwitz underneath a silver moon.
Euphoria ever too short-lived . . replaced with lead balloons.

It broke my soul to witness people torn from loved-one's hands.
Never chanced to say goodbye as guards screamed out demands.

(I . . was a great violinist. Perhaps you've heard of me?
Renowned throughout Vienna. Here - I'm just a detainee.)

Wails of the broken hearted echoed every day and night.
Sending prayers to absent Gods who'd failed us in our plight.

Not a day without the burnings. That vileness I still taste.
My music was the only thing that kept ME from such fates.

No childish laughter e'er befell our ears at Auschwitz Hell.
But I will be their voice worldwide. At Nuremberg as well.

Push that filth in his wheelchair. Let us watch HIM sweat.
Let his demons torture him. Make him pay his debt.

"My friend Bella"

My best friend Bella came today.
I love it when she comes to play.
My only friend that comes to call.
She's five, like me, but not as tall.

My mum gets cross, she says it's wrong.
She told me Bella don't belong.
I think it's cos I'm "pride and joy"
Why can't I have been a boy?

But I love her an' she loves me.
She used to live next door, you see.
But that was lots of years ago.
Where she moved to, I don't know.

She always wears a funny hat
that's made of tin; imagine that!
I think she's poor, her clothes aren't nice.
She wears a scary mask; and lies!

She doesn't even go to school!
Now even I know that's the rule.

Her daddy drowned in a sumbarine,
and her Uncle Ernie's really mean.

He's not her REAL uncle though.
But her mummy says they've got no dough.
She doesn't even have TV:
An' never paddled in the sea.

You see the lies and fibs she tells?
(And sometimes Bella really smells).
She says her house ain't got a bath.
I'm sorry but I had to laugh.

Then why does Bella make me sad?
Cos she's the only friend I've had.
I wish she DID live there, next door;
but that got bombed in the First World War!

Awww, its 6 o'clock, again she'll leave me.
No one in the world believes me.
She hears these sirens, SO she said!
Why's she crying, under my bed?

"The friend request"

A 'friend request' appeared one night, accepted cos he looked alright.
A handsome chap, in khaki greens (I think the yankee term's 'fatigues').

He messaged me a line or two. Was I married, kids? And all that poo!
All polite. Naught untoward. Hoped my words wouldn't leave him bored.

A dishy, fit, American, stationed in Afghanistan.
The boys, he said, are lonely there, and he was glad he'd ME to care.

We 'chatted' almost every night. He said, in darkness I was light.
He hated war and yearned to leave. He missed his kids. His wife he grieved.

He needed cash (the poor old thing) to get to see his kids an' kin.

It broke my heart to hear his woe, and just like him, my feelings grow.

Oh these brave, courageous, men! I made my mind up there and then.

I messaged him "cash on its way". And booked his flight to JFK.

(And as an extra special treat, I booked myself another seat.

He's gonna be so thrilled to meet me, I see a future, with Dimitri.)

I waited hours, 'til the penny dropped. Of course his pics were photoshopped.

(My family warned "don't be a jerk".) I tried his phone, that too didn't work.

Dimitri Alexander Tom. A major in the army.

(Major Tom, in other words. Yep I'm really barmy!)

He wasn't in Afghanistan or ever there in Syria.

Just a gang of conmen. Catfish from Nigeria!

The soldier boy

The soldier stood inside the room, wounded and forlorn.
A tranquil place, serene and bright. A haven from the norm.

People came towards him; open-armed and full of glee.
But unaware of how or why, he wept on bended knee.

A tender voice then spoke to him; a hand caressed his face.
"Thank you for your service boy now take your well earned place".

The soldier rose and looked around upon the congregation.
Cheers went up as crowds bestowed their heartfelt adoration.

'Twas then he noticed several pals, his comrades from the 'Stans.
And right behind the 'voice' that spoke, appeared his doting Grans.

He touched his wounded, bloody chest but felt no pain at all.
Euphoric and elated, standing strong his six feet tall.

The battle sounds had silenced now, replaced with love and joy.
Befitting for a hero such as this brave soldier boy.

He's here to stay. His deed is done. No chance for growing older.
Rest in peace eternally. Sleep softly sweet young soldier.

"In self-defence"

I bought myself a handgun from the gunsmith months ago.
I'm getting somewhat paranoid, this 'worry' will not go.
I did consider knives but just the thought fills me with dread.
Hence I keep this little pocket handgun by my bed.

My neighbourhood is dodgy. The youths are far 'too high'.
Crime-free nights in my street? Not a single one goes by.
They burgle, trash, and rampage. These louts show no remorse.
And IF they're caught, what happens then? NOTHING does, of course!

My nerves were shot to pieces but felt safer with my gun.
(I couldn't tell my kids that they've a crazy hair-brained mum).
I managed blissful slumber for at least a week or two,
until a dismal mishap (which you won't believe is true).

My son is in the forces, he's deployed for months on end.
His absence is a killer, and I miss my boy no end.
The party I've been planning when he's home again, on leave.
It's gonna be a huge surprise; one he won't believe!

Well I heard a distant creaking in the night, and then a click.
Frozen in my winceyettes, feeling ultra sick.
I reached for my new handgun and sat rigid 'neath the sheets.
The bedroom door burst open and I screamed and screamed and screamed.

There was such a rush and panic as the 'burglar' flailed about,
I think I scored a bulls-eye from the alto of his shout.
But my fear turned into horror as his painful cries begun,
and those words will ever haunt me "Why've you shot me mum?"

A flesh wound; nothing fatal. Nothing Dettol cannot cure.
(Throughout his life, I tell you, he's had so much worse before.)
But it's good to have my boy home tucked up safe inside his bed.
So I'll sell my gun tomorrow and I'll get a dog, instead.

"The gardening fork"

I broke my grandad's gardening fork whilst digging
yesterday.
I doubt it can be mended cos the tines have worn away.
I'll tell you now, it saddened me; I've had this fork for
years.
I sat down broken-hearted and admit I shed some tears.

I've had that fork for donkeys. It's never let me down.
I always reminisced of him when metal struck the ground.
His big strong arms, his muddy boots, sweat upon his brow.
He whistled as he worked the earth. Of him I was so proud.

His gardening tools he treasured. With those, he said, we'll
eat.
As long as God gives sun and rain, ask me - who needs
meat?
He weeded, dug, and toiled. He planted, watered, pruned.
His worldly capabilities could never be impugned.

'Old school' was my grandad. Before this world went
wrong.
Tormented thereinafter from his war years at The Somme.

Enlisted as a boy who wouldn't comprehend the horror:
Along with all the others who would never reap tomorrow.

I watched my lovely grandad as he whistled, while he worked.
(his nightmares, screams and sweats at night were latter things I learnt).
I learned a lot from watching him. I too respect the land.
Flora, fauna, water, air; together hand-in-hand.

But my garden fork's diminished and can't ever cultivate.
Redundant, useless, idle. Past its sell-by date.
So I'll bury it in the garden, and inter a little prayer,
with some of grandad's ashes, and a lock of grandma's hair.

"Payback time"

Treblinka. 1942. Worse than Hell if you're a Jew.
Me, my husband, daughter, son. Forced apart by a loaded gun.

I never saw my kin thereafter, or heard again their blissful laughter.
So in my heart I pledged revenge and swore to God they'd be avenged.

I was lucky. Ha! That's what they said, as they numbered me, and shaved my head.
Kept for 'fun' like an unpaid whore. The enemy in a battle-less war.

But then it changed one winter night. A brand new life. My heart took flight.
Oh no; not me. He's not MY spawn. The Aryan was a Lebensborn.

I nursed this child so pink and mild, and loved him like my own.
But he wasn't mine, and I schemed the crime when we were both alone.

(Josef was my firstborn. My darling, darling boy.
Annie was our daughter and her father's pride and joy.)

They shared no guilt or pity as they forced them to their fate
and I've had eighteen months or more to plan and contemplate.

Yes, I took their prized possession and I cut him, like we do.
I circumcised their 'treasure' and like me, he's now a Jew!

Oh they'll kill me now for certain but I honestly don't mind.
I'm euphoric in my vengeance cos for me, it's payback time.

"Fifty years and counting"

I've had this set of underwear for nigh on fifty years.
I bought it for a sweet young man, still wet behind the ears.

I was in my forties. He was just nineteen.
I think I taught him everything (you all know what I mean!)

His mother would've killed me, had she known where he was at.
(We never wasted any time with meaningless chit chat!)

Oh the fun, the thrill, the passion! Pure erotic lust.
In the office after dark, or the barn in the hay an' dust.

A fine young soldier laddie. I grieved when he went to war.
I gave that boy a will to live and a promise to return home, for.

.

Did he come back? No one told me. Never saw neither hide nor hair.
(I heard he went to Burma… not a picnic there!)

It was silk. Lilac and lacy. It won't fit me any how!
I keep it for the memories. They're all I'm left with . . . now.

"Haunted"
A Short Story

As Harry put the handset back on the cradle, he felt the familiar heavy-heartedness envelope him. It had been over ten years since he'd heard the first mention of her name; Ingrid. And ten years of trying to forget HOW. His sister, Fern, had telephoned to say that Ingrid was arriving at the weekend and could he collect her from the station? Ingrid. Bert's "wunderschöne Schwester" (beautiful sister).

1930 had been a non-descript year so far. He'd been one of the 'lucky' ones to return to the safe shores of Blighty - 'home'. Though in truth he'd never really left THERE. Did any of them? Ypres was where he woke up every morning, and it was where he lay his head at night. The bloody killing fields drawing him back whilst he fitfully tried to find peace within the confines of his utility sheets and his candlewick bedspread. His four walls offered no protection against the echoing screams of his pals as they succumbed to the enemy's barrage of bullets. Sleep eluded him. Always. The phone call had been unsettling and transported him back to Hell.

Harry was then just 18. A sniper. The best of the best. The creme-de-la-creme. He never missed his target though he prayed to the Lord Almighty, he would. He would inwardly beg his targets to move. "Please bend down to tie up your boot and live another day". He hated killing, and cursed his immaturity for enlisting before his call up. But, like most, he felt the need to dutifully serve his country. Such foolishness of the young..

He went into his bedroom to retrieve the photograph. A sepia photograph he'd treasured. The only good memory to take from No Man's Land. Christmas Day, 1914. The truce! How is one supposed to feel? How is one able to express that trepidation, the anxiety, that FEAR? One isn't.

1914: Bert was a barber from Essen, in Germany, and was providing shaves and haircuts in exchange for an English cigarette. He'd wanted to join in with his Waffenbrüder (brothers in arms) playing football, but he had a queue of 'roll-ups' to be earned so he figured he'd forfeit showing off his mastery footwork on the mock-up football pitch and humour his waiting tobacco clientele with his effervescent personality whilst at the same time rattling away in a language nobody in his queue understood but laughed alongside him anyway, whilst he made his 'enemies' look and feel a little more human again; for a while. He could've shed so much blood, with his blade...

He showed his 'new found friends' a photograph. "Sie ist Ingrid. Meine wunderschöne Schwester". (This is Ingrid. My beautiful sister.) We all agreed Bert's girlfriend was a beauty! A surreal Christmas day. A whole universe away from the grim reality of the present AND of the unforeseeable future.

Harry didn't remember how they all ended up back in the trench. His last recollection was laughing till his sides hurt because Bert had cut his own finger whilst shaving someone (he couldn't remember who) and got blood everywhere. At least that's what he thought he'd remembered. So when Bert suddenly appeared in front of him, at the top of HIS trench, he hesitated. That minuscule of a second's realisation (but felt like a lifetime) as Harry, already trembling and feeling a loosening of his bowels; prepared, aimed, locked eyes, and fired... and the two - who'd laughed heartily together only hours before, in a language neither could understand but did -- fell. And the world, too, fell silent around them . . . Harry saw the cracked sepia photograph of Bert's 'Schwester' sticking up from his pocket. And he took it.

Heidelberg 1919. How he was to negotiate his way around these foreign cities, towns, streets, he had no idea! "Why can't everything be in English?" With the help of the Red Cross it had taken only 11 months to locate Ingrid Ochs. She'd moved to Heidleberg after the war. She couldn't stay in Essen. It was too painful. So much loss, so much heartache.

After losing both her parents in a bombing, and her only brother in Ypres (Belgium), Heidelberg was going to be a new beginning. She was leaving Essen and its memories in a sealed box never to be reopened. Pain was an unwelcome guest. No one wanted to prolong its stay.

Harry managed to get the gist of using the telephone inside his hotel, with the help of a man who reminded him of a German Officer they'd captured. He wondered what HIS part of the war was. How many Englishmen had HE slaughtered, dismembered, imprisoned, persecuted, tortured? The list ticked on in his mind. He pictured him in his Nazi uniform and his stomach tightened as he fought the urge to spit in his face. Images of his buddies, young and old, screaming in agony, the sounds of gunfire screeching and blasting; and sweat trickled down his face as he tried desperately to remind himself that it was over. Over. But it wasn't. It isn't. It would never be. So through gritted teeth he forced "vielen dank". (Many thanks).

He knew that Bert's girlfriend was a beauty. It was obvious not only in the photograph that he'd shown everyone but in the way his face had lit up when he spoke of her that day. That Christmas Day, 1914. The 'cigarette' queue had been drooling. And there she was now. Sitting right in front of him. Ingrid. (Why, oh why, does the world not speak in the same tongue?) Harry found himself sat in front of Bert's 'Schwester'. His SISTER!

She was agitated; wanted to know all the why's and wherefores of this intrusion. She was unwavering and steadfast. They were enemies, this man and her brother. Why was he stalking her? It was unfathomable that they were sitting here together; Englishman and German woman, face to face, in a little cafe in Heidelberg, smoking and drinking tea.

And it was in this sad little cafe that belied all Harry had come to Germany for. His secret would remain within the muddy, rat-infested, Hell-on-Earth trenches of No Man's

Land till he breathed his last breath. The war was over. (But his battle would never be.)

The truth choked him, so invented some sorry story about finding her brother wounded and took him to receive medical treatment; he had wanted to return the photograph he'd found in Bert's pocket. She'd believed him. And actually THANKED him! He cringed. They exchanged addresses and corresponded. Often.

The two sisters of the two enemies, became good friends after Fern had asked if she might write to Ingrid, too. Pen friends initially and then progressed with phone calls until one summer Ingrid invited Fern to Heidelberg to stay for a couple of weeks. It became a regular thing with both of them crossing the channel for frequent liaisons. Harry felt that he and Bert could've been good friends. But they were destined to be mortal enemies.

A split second. That's all it took. A split second to haunt a man for eternity.

Part Six: We Do Love Our Animals

No book, poetry or otherwise, written by someone of British origin, would be complete without including some mention of their pets. Dogs in particular are special in the UK. People take them everywhere, including to their "local" (which we Americans would know as a pub). Dogs are trained to wait patiently underneath a table while their owner socializes. Dogs are even seen briefly tied to the equivalent of a canine hitching post outside of High Street shops and no one bats an eye.

Cats, on the other hand, are a different story. My personal experience while living in the agricultural setting of the "North of England" suggested that cats were for vermin control. They weren't afforded the special "member of the family" status that dogs were. Cats were largely outdoor animals. Their contribution was keeping rats, mice, and rabbits at bay.

Once again, Lisa does an admirable job describing how she feels about and is impacted by pets – her own or those of other people. She even uses personification as a means to describe how a mistreated dog might feel.

"Reasons why I'm single"

The cat shat on my outside mat, it really was a stinker.
I almost put my foot in it: the dirty little tinker!

I had to throw that mat away; no way I'm gonna clean it!
I swear he does it one more time he's dead (an' YES I mean it!)

Everyday he tears around - his routine mad rendition.
He claws my legs, he bites my toes; I scream into submission!

He hates the dog, the dog hates him. They tease each other daily.
The cat's called Cat (just simply that), the Labrador's named Bailey.

Now Bailey is a brilliant boy; a gorgeous, placid mutt.
A treasure in my golden years: Cat is anything but!

Take Sunday last, for instance; I'd a 'guest' for Sunday lunch.
I'd got salmon on the drainer and I'd made a potent Punch.

Well Cat jumped on the drainer, got the salmon in his paws.
Hurled it in the air . . and it landed in his jaws!

And AS he toyed, that ruddy cat fair sent my Punch Bowl crashing.
Bailey started lapping up, he found it really smashing.

So I had to get a take-away to feed my 'special' guest.
Then Bailey started breaking wind (I think you'll guess the rest!)

He started retching, violently. First vomit then diarrhoea.
The guy just left, was clear he had no chance of getting near.

So that was that, it's best to live the single life I've made
cos Cat and dog ensure I've not a chance of getting laid.

"Chained up"

I know you hear me every day
yet still you turn your head away.
Help me rid this cold steel chain.
I want to feel alive again.

It's been like this for five long years.
No-one feels my pain or fears.
I'm left alone each day to wallow.
Drenched in sadness each tomorrow.

For boys round here, I'm easy prey
cos I can't fight, nor get away.
Un-doctored too, (no cash to splash),
my babies killed and dumped like trash.

I miss them all (and so would you,
if you endured this torture too).
No nursing done, no farewell kiss.
Read my plea. Remember this!

My human folk, they do not care;
they've never walked me anywhere.
Winter, summer, rain or shine,
'imprisoned' on this chain of mine.

You know I'm here, you hear my bark;
morning, noon, and through the dark.
The parasites that fill my bed,
these ticks and fleas, are better fed.

I'm begging you to hear my cry,
and not to turn the same 'blind eye'.
Free me from this cold steel chain.
Help me BE a dog again.

"Not my dog"

The next door neighbour's dog is here, sleeping like a log.
Let me just reiterate, he IS the neighbour's dog!
He seems to think he lives here. Morning, noon, and night.
He eats me out of house and home. I ought to put him right!

He doesn't even NEED a key, he lets his daft self in!
And I'm as much a ruddy fool, patronising him!
I'll have to set some boundaries. He needs to give a toss.
I'll wake him up and kick him out; show him who's the boss.

So I dangled some old bacon that was causing quite a whiff;
underneath his nostrils hoping this would prompt a sniff.
He didn't move a muscle so I poked him in the ribs.
But then I felt damn guilty cos I hated doing this.

But he has got another home, where there he's also fed!
So why on Earth is he still thinking my duvet's his bed?
And even when it's raining it is here he comes to shake,
muddy splashes everywhere, his neck I wanna break.

Tho really he's a darling and he gives me such big licks,
Unfortunately he's too daft to do the simplest tricks.
He barks at nothing visual, and he often looks forlorn.
But wags his tail, (I yell and flail) when digging up my lawn!

So I'll leave the mutt to slumber as I tiptoe by his side.
Then suddenly he turns to me with brown eyes open wide!
I guiltily apologise for ruining his nap:
Cos after all is said and done, I love this dear sweet chap!

"One flew over the cockatoo's nest"

My mother is a fan of birds, she loves our feathered friends.
Budgies, pigeons, thrushes, crows: Peacocks, ducks and
hens.

She loves the morning chorus when the birds sing from the
trees.
Spends hours watching Martens build their nests around
our eaves.

We've little 'houses' here and there, and families come
each year.
And should she find a fledgling dead, I've watched her
shed a tear.

She loves our household cats and dogs but knew she'd love
a bird.
So I thought I'd buy a Mynah. They're great talkers, so I've
heard.

Her birthday was approaching so I searched the Internet.
Couldn't find a breeder, so consulted with our vet.

He likewise knew no breeders but "would she like a
cockatoo?"
I nearly slapped him in the face! My mother's 92!

Red-faced and so embarrassed I acknowledged, yes, she
might.
10 weeks old and both wings clipped to save from taking
flight.

My mother was delighted and she vowed she'd make him
talk.

He'd sit on mother's shoulder but for months he'd only
squawk!

A ruddy Grand it cost me but she'd thanked me endlessly.
She said she hadn't known the joy a cockatoo could be!

And Cocky started learning. He could 'bark' and he could
'meow'.
He'd 'cuckoo' with the cuckoo clock, the phone 'rang'
every hour!

I also grew to love that bird; mimic extraordinaire.
. . and one day I found Frankie . . . an' Cocky's feathers
everywhere!

Part Seven: Love, Lust, and Nuance

Love is a very complicated emotion that takes many forms. It is so complicated that the Ancient Greeks had six unique words to describe love and its variations. Ranging from a religious interpretation to courtesies and hospitality, these words are so diverse in meaning that volumes have been written to explain them.

Philautia, a love for one's own happiness or advantage, fits nicely into Maslow's "Hierarchy of Needs." But… (and it is a BIG "but") it can also be described as the moral flaws of vanity and selfishness. In its extremes, *philautia* can be either self-compassion or self-obsession.

Storge is the love and affection between parents and their children. It means acceptance of family members, regardless of how weird or dysfunctional they might be. It is a common, natural empathy.

Eros describes the love of sexual passion. Socrates argued that *eros* aspires for the spiritual plane of existence without completely focusing on the corporeal. Over time, the lustful component of *eros* evolves into an appreciation of beauty within another person.

Philia is an affectionate regard between equals. Aristotle described it as a loyalty to friends and community. It is a dispassionate, virtuous love.

Xenia describes the concept of hospitality within the framework of generosity and courtesy. It is a more ritualistic form of love expressed as a reciprocal relationship between a guest and host. *Xenia* also applies to the hospitality shown to those who are far from home.

The most enduring form of love, according to Ancient Greek philosophers, is *agape.* Christians equate *agape* to the unconditional love of God for his children.

Lisa's poems and short story in this section cover the entire range of "love." From the manifestations of lust through the unconditional love of *agape*, and even the loss of love, there is something for everyone.

"Before you meet the handsome Prince"

Oh ugly toad there, in my pond.
Regally perched on my lily frond.
I ponder if the fable's true?
Should I try an' capture you?

I hear your calling in the dawn,
(not unlike a ship's foghorn),
A mating call? A slimy croak?
Or in disguise my longed-for bloke?

So I made a fish net from my stocking.
Oh pretty please, is this so shocking?
If folklore's true an' bag my prize,
my stocking top's his least surprise!

I cast my rod, I lured him in;
chuckling at my brazen sin.
Then laid him on my clean duvet,
soon I'll have my Prince to lay.

Oh those fairy tales I've read.
And now Prince Charming's on my bed!
I bathed, then dressed in jewels and lace
anticipating true love's face.

I took his bulbous form in palms,
I stroked his back, his head, his arms.
Savoured all, embracing this . .
then planted that iconic kiss.

I retched at first and then I spit!
Goodness grief he tastes like s**t!
An' the magic didn't work, you see . .
it wasn't HIM! It was a SHE!

147

"The biggest fan"

I doubt that you'll remember me. But I remember you.
It was almost fifteen years ago, when you casually said
"how do?"

I'm stood outside 'The Albert' waiting at the taxi line.
You, in jeans and tee shirt looking gorgeously divine.

Your dark eyes so beguiling I hung on to every word.
This 16 year old innocent naive to the big wide world.

Did you know I bought your albums, had your poster on
my wall?
I fantasied I'd marry you. Your biggest fan of all.

I'd practise in the mirror singing all your songs with you.
When I heard you're due in London I felt all my dreams
come true.

I worked hard to buy the ticket, (costing almost sixty
pounds).
Worked mornings noons an' evenings doing several paper
rounds.

I did errands for the neighbours, did it all to meet my idol.
If I'd missed my chance to see you I thought I'd be
suicidal.

Then I heard you sing, I watched you dance,
mesmerised in a whirlwind trance.
I prayed this night wouldn't end at all.
Bereft at the final curtain call.

And that's when you approached me. A broad grin on your face.
Before I knew what happened we'd arrived outside 'my place'.

You'd gone before the dawning with my innocence defiled.
A broken heart and a part of you so casually left behind.

Oh so many years ago: but you're back again I see.
Do you know we have a daughter? Can you remember me?

"The phone-call"

Hello Clare, it's me.

Doubt that you will know me, but we share a love, you see.

Oh! He hasn't told you? I can't say I'm surprised.

Well I'm calling now to tell you of your lover's wicked lies.

I smelt perfume on his clothing and I found your long blonde hair.

And in his sleep he calls your name: wrapped around ME, Clare!

I know that dreams are more than strange, I truly understand.

But I've seen signs for ages now: our future's in your hands.

I followed him last night, you see. Praying I was wrong.

But all it did was reaffirm I WAS right . . all along.

You both pulled in that car park. You left yours an' went to his.

I tell you Clare it broke my heart to watch you lovers kiss.

I'd our daughter in the backseat. (Sleeping in her chair).
Did you know your lover has a baby daughter, Clare?
I feel sure he hasn't told you like he's not told me of you!
Now you know his secret, the rest is up to you!

I don't blame you for an instant. I too, fell for his charms.
He wooed ME with his boyish grin, I melted in his arms.
I loved him to the moon and back; he said he loved me too.
My stomach churns to know, no doubt, he says the same to you.

I found your number in his phone. (Don't tell him that I know).
I'm calling you, no, begging you, to let my husband go.
Let my daughter know her dad at least 'til she's at school.
After that I promise you, you're welcome to my fool.

Signed, with love . . . "

I plucked a feather from my wing and felt a pain-like thrill.
Took a sharpened blade to make a perfect writing quill:
then dipped it in the magic ink, and hovered for a while.
Words came flooding fast and now at last I'll make him smile.

I had to make the words profound; I couldn't let him down.
To right a wrong I made before and turn his life around.
I'd missed his chance for true romance, the ball was in my court.
Again I must administer the lessons I've been taught.

The school insists the students use the arrow and the bow.
to help our targets find true love; their destinies we show.
I don't uphold such violence though the rules dictate I should.
I believe it should be speech, cos WORDS are understood.

I did try tested measures but my aim was way off cue
so his lover ran for cover cos she didn't have a clue.
But now the Boss has given me a chance to make amends.
My script, I hope will reunite them more than 'just good friends'.

My feathered quill is ready with a magic to impart.
Tailored words perfected from the feelings of his heart.
I shot the written script I penned and winged them to her phone.
Her face alights, her heart takes flight. NOW the seed's been sown.

I may still be a novice but I'm glad I broke the habit.
(As the saying goes there're many ways to skin a rabbit)
And everyone's assured me that this time I scored a hit.
The rest is up to them to make it all a perfect fit.

Update . . .

I took a peek a week ago, to check if yes or no!
Rewarded by The Master with a gold string to my bow.
He sat with me to watch the lovers' home erupt with laughter.
Satisfied the end's in sight for "Happy Ever After".

"The bottom line"

It's hard for me to write the words, these words that say 'goodbye'.
You'll read them when you're home tonight, and beg the question "why"?

And you won't find any answers. Indeed I found none, too.
The bottom line, and truth be told, I'm not in love with you.

Oh I tried to be a good wife. I tried for many years.
And though you weren't the one at fault t'was I who shed the tears.

I'd be lonely in a crowded room, with you there by my side.
Everybody having fun; my anguish I would hide.

You never knew though, did you? You never 'felt' my lies.
You never saw my cowardice or questioned my disguise.

I lied and cheated daily, feigning love and happiness.
But all the time it was an act, a painful sad duress.

Of course I loved you first off. I was proud of you; in awe.
Together we were perfect and I wished for nothing more.

We were young, and life was simple. I grew up, but oh not you.
And every single day you made me cringe at things you'd do.

We've reached the bottom line, you see. My sanctitude has gone.
'Goodbye' is now the only word to right where we went wrong.

"Til we meet again"

Hello my dear old buddy: I hear you've not been well.
I sympathise and empathise; this getting old lark's Hell.

They tell me things are pretty rough and your end is nigh in
sight.
So I'm sending you these memories, which I hope you'll
read tonight.

I wanted to remind you of the 'good old days' of ours.
The days when we were young and brave, and earned our
battle scars.

The youngsters now won't comprehend the traumas we
went through.
Fighting, screaming, killing, fearing. Lies and secrets too.

But then the nightmare ended. Well, perhaps it did for
some.
But you and I will ever mourn the cost of Victory won.

Did you my friend, remember! Cos I have; every day.
I'm sure like me, the past has never been a breath away.

I was injured, shot and wounded. Left for dead, no doubt.
Torpedoed by the nazis. An' body parts all about.

The ice cold water hurt my bones, I felt myself slip under.
You held me up, like a lover would. Not just a naval
number.

We made it home though buddy. We married; tarried on.
You with Mu, had a kid or two, and I, with my Yvonne.

The last time that I saw you was in 1962. You sobbed and said you loved me,
I said "I love you too".

We kept our secret all these years. Oh to again begin.
And to be as young in this age boy, when love now's not a sin.

So I'm here to say goodbye to you: my hero of all men.
And I pray to God that it's my time soon,
so that we can meet again.

"Til death do us part"

And then it all fell into place.
Her beauty and obvious grace.
You've replaced me I see; an' that's tragic for me
to see happiness on your smug face.

Is she naughty, flirty, dirty?
Does she make you beg for more?
Do you whisper that you love her
an' you never felt this way before?

I tried hard to be pleased, but I'm not.
Jealousy festers like rot.
It's not been yet a year since you last shed a tear
and I guess you've not missed me a jot.

You know she isn't perfect, cos her teeth come out at
night.
And on her bum and thighs I've seen a ton of cellulite.

You must know that I know, cos you see,
our home doesn't smell now, of me.
I see nothing of mine, but I see the white line
on your hand where a ring used to be.

*Yes! THAT gold ring which bound us when we both
declared "I do".*
The one that cost a fortune I had specially made for you!

It was ME who held strings to your heart.

Fell in love with you right from the start

How we danced to our song, and we'd laugh all night long,

now your new love has taken my part.

Everything's forgotten now you have somebody new.
But I won't rest in peace because revenge is overdue.

I hate this new love that you've found.

Should be ME that you're arms are around.

I hear you two lovers, make love under covers,

(but you'll never hear me make a sound.)

So I'll taunt you, haunt you, scare you,
I will be there, everywhere.
It's not my nature to be such a hater,
but you'll rue the day . . I swear.

It wasn't my fault I fell ill.

And honey, I'm here for you still.

It's because you don't grieve, that I'm not gonna leave.

Ask me nicely and maybe I will!

So you thought since I'm dead, you'd be free?

Did you think I'd relent easily?

I won't let her sleep tight when you're curled up at night

I will drive her away, you DAMN SHITE!

"The new guy"

There's a new guy just moved in next door.
He's really quite a dish!
Muscled, tanned, and handsome.
I'd say he's 50'ish?

I've yet to introduce myself,
I daren't appear too keen.
Perhaps I'll take a bottle round?
Good neighbourly . . I mean.

The house next door's been empty now
for nigh on three decades.
I might go round this afternoon
in shorts and Ray Ban shades.

Take some fruit grown from my garden,
a way to get acquainted.
Perfumed to the eyeballs
and my face and toe nails painted.

(I even hung some thongs out on my clothes-line . .
yesterday,
some stockings and suspenders and a black lace negligee.)

As I waved across the garden wall
beaming pearly whites,
he blanked me very rudely.
So I scuttled back inside!

I'm sure you've guessed what's coming next.
I feel a total dick
cos lying right beside him
was his dog . . and a white cane stick!

© 2020 Lisa Talbott

"The final, FINAL goodbye"

I've said it oh so many times, I'll say it once again.
I'm gonna MEAN goodbye this time, and free myself of
men!

I've yearned a skid-free toilet where the seat is always
down.
A laundry just for my stuff. No Y-fronts to be found.

I want to watch a weepy film, and wallow in sad thoughts.
(I'm not a fan of football, rugby, boxing, or such sports).

I love my king size antique bed, my vintage crocheted
sheets:
(Preferably in silence without snores or sweaty feet.)

I'd love champagne for breakfast in a proper crystal flute.
(Instead I get a MUG of tea, staring at some brute!)

Cultured dinner parties; classic music, and the arts.
(Not belching after pie an' chips and guffaws after farts!)

A restaurant in Soho with some Chateau Neuf de Pape.
(To him, a treat's McDonalds with some chicken nugget
crap!)

Take me to the movies, or the opera, or the Ritz.
(He likes nights on my chaise lounge with beers and porno
discs!)

I've a wardrobe full of Prada that no soul has seen me in.
(Reebok trainers, Calvin Klein's, are his, but not my,
thing!)

Oh I've tried the subtle hinting but he's cocked the same deaf ear.
I need to get him out my hair before he takes root here!

I did consider murder but I KNOW I can't go there.
I'm sure there must be some daft bint who'd snap him up . . . somewhere??

See, the straw that broke the camels back was just an hour ago.
Anticipating flowers and gifts . . . He claimed he didn't know!

So I packed his bag, his laundry too, and left it in the shed.
A little card, inscribed inside with "adios, Dickhead".

Enjoying now my birthday and relieved I've been so strong.
Remote's all mine, the night's divine, and peace with a gin and ton!

"I'm a hero!"

Oh I really have to tell you all what happened yesterday!
I'm feeling quite excited here, so let me have my say.

I 'thought' I'd met a lovely guy, a real-live gentle man!
I guessed he must be single cos I sneaked at his left hand.

I'd just popped into Aldi (and before you have to ask,
Yes, I'd kept my distance, and of course I wore my mask!)

Shopping is my thrill these days, the only place I go.
The stores are void of people and there's not a lot on show.

But I went to buy a pumpkin cos I thought I'd bake a pie.
Was down the produce section when I guess I caught his
eye.

He asked for my opinion on the types of two bananas.
Should he buy organic or the cheaper, from Bahamas?

He held my gaze for longer than I deemed was necessary.
My cheeks began to sweat and my face reddened like a
berry.

I knew he must be flirting but I stuttered, truth be told.
(Occurrences like this are rare when one becomes this old!)

In honesty I felt some guilt, I'd passed the guy my number.
And sexily I teased him bagging carrots and cucumber!

Well I left him to his choice and joined the queue to pay
my bill.
And as I'm loading up I saw his hands inside the till!

If I hadn't got my mask on you'd mistake my fear for
laughin'
And Aldi, in this crisis, hadn't ONE security staff in.

I launched my pumpkin at his head, he went down for the
count.
I've now been hailed a hero: such heroics though I doubt.

My face is on the tele and revered now near and far.
The junta here presented me a brand new motorcar!

And Aldi have insisted that I never pay a thing.
So my house is bulging at the seams with vodka, rum, and
gin.

It's too abrupt, I hear you say. This ending isn't right.
Indeed it is: I bailed him out and meeting him tonight.

"Delete"

It has taken me a decade. Ten whole lonely years:
to wipe away each memory an' erase a million tears.

I called your number often. Your voice would make me
smile.
Always late at night in bed, to talk with you a while.

Of course you never answered. I got your answer tone.
I left so many messages to no one there at home.

It's time I oughta let you go, my grieving should be done.
Would you have grieved as long for me? I doubt you
would've, Hon.

I'll keep the cards you sent me but your number has to go.
So I scroll up really quickly, then scroll down real slow.

There's your name and number. And this moment's
bittersweet.
I kiss goodbye, breakdown and cry, and then I hit
DELETE.

"The Jaguar Tie Pin"
A Short Story

The Motor Show in Germany was fascinating. I wouldn't have missed it for the World. Not that I'm ultra fanatical about fast cars: I just love the ambience, the adrenalin, and enthusiasm of those who do. Speed actually worries me. I'm a creature of habit: preferring the tranquility of driving slowly, round country roads, with a full tank, and everything legal about the vehicle I drive. And appreciating the view as I'm driving along. But hey… call me old fashioned.

So when Dot asked me if I fancied earning a bit of extra cash, in the office, that afternoon, I was all ears. Good old Dot. It'll be fun, she said. It's the bank holiday so we don't need to book holiday time off work. We'll get the train to meet the guys who're doing the show out there, and we get paid! (She ACTUALLY said "I'm gonna get paid for getting laid". But I didn't tell you that!) Sounds fantastic! Germany here we come!

Oh my! It certainly was fun. The ferry crossing was horrendous but hey, once we got over our seasickness and arrived at our hotel and had a few wines, we were *"Guten Tag"* ready. The next morning, albeit still quite sickly, we set up our wares, ready for the exhibition, with all the F1 racing paraphernalia you could imagine. T-shirts, badges, scarfs, model cars; and Dot and I we were dressed to impress these gorgeous krauts that were very willing to part with their hard earned Marks. Some were ever more willing to part with a lot more than their Deutsch marks too, and Dot and I were only to happy to oblige. Bratwurst sausages and Liebfraumilch, and smokey nightclubs, became our bank holiday favourites.

One of the things The Motor Show got me thinking about, was when I struggled getting into, and out of, the very famous Bat-mobile, the Camel car, and other F1 works of magnificence. 8 stone[1] wet through and boy did I have difficulty! How do these guys do it? Bravo!

But the lights go out, the clock ticks on, and time and tide wait for no man. Hence, we missed the damn train back home. But did Dot and I care? No! Still high on the delights of Germany and a million photos to look back on in our dotage, we savoured these next hours and reminisced who we'd kissed, and to whom we promised to come back to Frankfurt again. Such tarts! "One last photo Dot, of you

---

[1] A "stone" is a British colloquial unit of weight equal to approximately 14 pounds and was at one time a standard measurement for a quantity of wool sheared from a sheep. "8 stone" would be roughly 112 pounds.

looking like a homeless person at St Pancras". And THAT's when HE appeared! How very dare he? An intruder in our memory!

He just slung his sweet cute face right into my focus! My camera clicked. His pearly whites gleamed. I wanted to KILL him! Oh, of course it was hilarious - they decided. He and his friend had also missed their last train home, so it was perfectly natural to amuse themselves by annoying others. I'm lying. It was a welcome annoyance. Does that make sense?

S'funny isn't it, how you go from wanting to kill someone, to suddenly seeing them as a potential father for your future unborn children? Not that I wanted children, you understand! But… It's 7.30 a.m. and Andy's train is about to leave. (Don't go, please don't go!). So I gave him the Jaguar tie pin I'd 'salvaged' from the packing up of the Grand Prix memorabilia to keep as a memento of a great experience. "I'll call you" he shouted, as he boarded his train out of St Pancras. (Picture me running at the side of his window. Pretending my heart's breaking.)

I'll never see him again. Of course not! It was just one of those 'brief encounters'. Something to look back on when you see these pics you've taken. And you'll remember. But I did! I did see him again. Many many times.

However, once a bitch, always a bitch, and I broke that lovely man's heart. "Andy, I'm sorry. I tried to tell you. I tried to find you, too, but you moved away. I couldn't find you. I tried." Getting old is a privilege not afforded to all. We reflect and reminisce. We wonder what life could've been, and what you're doing now.

So I tried once more on Facebook. Kicking myself because I know he isn't on there. I tried for years. Many years, he'll never know. But today! Today's different. I found him!I found him - and then I had to Google him cos I couldn't believe what I found. I found him. But I lost him. Lost him to Hollywood! There he is in major films. He's married too, with kids.

I won't send him a friend request. He'll not remember me. I will be that wicked reminder of a lucky escape, but really shouldn't he be thankful? I tortured myself tonight, watching his interview on American TV. His familiar smile. The way he folded his hands. Of course, he won't remember me. So I go to switch him off. Again. And that's when I realised that we don't really ever forget our past.

There's MY Andy. Dressed to kill in a white shirt and black suit. Telling the world of the films he's made. His tie is blue. I noticed. He's wearing a Jaguar tie pin…

Part Eight: It's Five O'Clock Somewhere

Consumption of alcohol is a generally social activity. When in moderation, having a drink with one's mates after work is an expression of camaraderie and a uniquely social occasion. In extremes, consumption of alcohol can affect lives and devastate relationships in so many different ways.

Once again, Lisa describes the good and the bad sides of alcohol. She talks about social drinking. She talks about the dire consequences of excess. She even talks about how distasteful someone of a different persuasion might find a socially-acceptable situation that involves alcohol.

I am sure we can all see ourselves in at least one of of the poems in this section.

"Reasons why I drink"

I bought myself a scratch card with a euro that I found.
(My eyes are always searching streets for treasures on the
ground).
Hence I'm feeling really lucky, so I tried to hedge my bets;
and I got myself a scratch card whilst I went for cigarettes.

Now, I'VE not had what one could call a charmed an' easy
life.
It's been hard work and filled with many years of bloomin'
strife!
But my card turned out a winner and I laughed out loud,
with glee.
I'd gone and won three euros: so I bought another three!

I'm stood inside that Offy, and start scratching at those
squares.
Chuckling like a loony whilst ignoring people's stares.
But Lady Luck's still on my side, she's waved her magic
wand
cos bits of silver scratchings now reveal I've won a grand!

Ooh I'm dancing and I'm laughing, I just can't believe my wealth.

So to celebrate my fortune grabbed some good stuff off the shelf!

The top one, not the bottom that my usual funds dictate.

And I'm gonna do the lotto too cos who knows what's my fate?

That Chardonnay was gorgeous and I drank not one but two.

And this morning I'm surrounded with my last night's vindaloo.

'Twas then that I remembered I'd logged on to Camelot.

Specifying numbers - just before I lost the plot.

Well would you ruddy 'Christmas Eve', Behold this millionaire!

Write your begging letters friends and pledge how much you care.

I'll log on now and get those millions winging my sweet way.

Oh God! What's this? Press send, complete?

DAMN that Chardonnay!

"Insomnia"

One o'clock. Two o'clock. Three o'clock. Four!
Counting sheep and sleeping pills don't do it any more.

Stayed up late, watched Dinner Date, read books to try 'n chill.
I've done the lot, I jest ye not, but sleep eludes me still.

I've walked the dog, I tried to jog, before I climb the stairs.
I've stopped the cheese, I'm all at ease, I've even said me prayers.

So why do I not sleep at night and always wide awake?
I NEED my forty winks because I'm tired for goodness sake!

And then a pal passed on advice, a tip that's great for sleep.
"Get y'self some gin and ton and pour it - finger deep".

Well why did I not think of that? Of course it all made sense!
So eight o'clock last night I tell ya I was right incensed!

I practised out the finger test and wow, went down a treat.
So much so that later on I poured it out just neat.

I ginned s'more, and smelt the floor. I'd lost the plot by then.
No clue of time, was all sublime, it's fourpence after ten?

What a floozy! Feeling woozy, ooh, I wanna cry.
Stomach churning. House is turning. Please God let me die.

I thus attest the method best - advise it? I shall not!
The reason found I slept so sound? A hangover, that's what.

Christmas Eve Past"

The mistletoe has perished. The holly berries gone.
The Christmas tree's redundant; posthumously forlorn.

Presents left unopened. Christmas cards unread.
Sunlight streams through dirty windows taunting me with
dread.

"Just one more" you whispered to the barmaid, with a
wink.
"It's Christmas only once a year let's all have one last
drink".

I knew you'd had too many. I knew it hours before.
That 'last' drink you had was two, then three, then four.

You wouldn't leave the car there though I begged and
pleaded to.
So I was just as much to blame for sitting next to you.

Flashing lights and sirens encompassed our Christmas Eve.
A nightmare unrealistic for the seasonal make-believe.

Your funeral . . You'd have loved it. Your drunken pals all
came!
A real-life carbon copy of our Christmas Eve again.

Sunlight streams through dirty windows. Ask me, do I
care?
I see it but I leave it an' just stare from my wheelchair.

"Everybody's different"

Don't invite me to your party cos I'll say I'll come, but
won't.
I'll pretend I'm all excited . . but it's the last thing that I
want.

I won't join you all for drinks at night when the office
closes up.
So go ahead, enjoy yourselves; I hate a crowded pub.

Nightclubs are a nightmare, and restaurants make me
sweat.
My heart starts pounding in a crowd an' that's what folk
don't get.

I KNOW I'm anti-social; it's a stigma I endure.
I participated years ago: Don't want to any more.

I adore my peace and quiet. Isolation is my choice.
Myself, the only one to please, to heed my inner voice.

I don't mean to be offensive and I hope you'll understand
Text me, mail me, write a line: Normality I can't stand.

It's the joy of doing nothing and the bliss of solitude,
that far surpasses all the guilt I get for seeming 'rude'.

So don't make me make excuses because be sure I will decline.
My comfort zone's my haven and it's where I walk the line.

"My last wish"

Has my final wish come true?
'cos I wished really hard, for you.
I wished that you could make it 'home'
so I won't have to die, alone.

Are you driving; on your way?
Will you make it here, today?
I know we've not seen eye-to-eye
and really, does it matter why?

But beg you now for this last chance
for absolution (in advance)
and remind you of our early years
with no false pity or crocodile tears.

Oh I missed you endlessly:
and wondered why you hated me.
Yes I was a naive fool . .
. . reactive of a worthless tool!

But the blame cannot be all my fault
cos you were like a lightning bolt.
Bones would mend but blows didn't end,
cos alcohol was your best friend.

I've wished you here to right our wrongs
and clear the air of our bygones.
I heard you then: your words still chill.
Banded loud, like overkill.

But forget it now cos all is gone.
I don't expect to keep you long.
I'm sick, and want to make a truce instead.
So I'll see you in Hell . . just like you said!

.

Part Nine: In the Rearview Mirrors of Life

Aging is full of surprises. Memory lapses. Vision deficiencies. Death. The list goes on and on. In this segment, Lisa manages to evoke a range of emotions – from humor to grief and sympathy – in several poems that focus on aging and the challenges we all face as our birthdays accumulate.

Try as we might, stopping the parade of aging is impossible. We try to hide it. We cover things up. We color it. Anything we can do to conceal our aging from the world.

Meanwhile, memory issues caused by degenerative conditions such as Alzheimer's affect not only the victim, but those around them as well. The victim is often not aware of current time and place; instead, their memories transport them to another time in their life. One day, it might be the victim's teenage years; the next, it might be a significant life event like marriage or the birth of a child. There might even be lucid days in the current moment; these days need to be cherished.

Unlike the fog of Alzheimers, reminiscences of days gone by and "what could have been" can be uplifting, especially if the memory is a pleasant one. Lisa writes about those moments as well, in an inimitably poignant fashion.

"Step backwards"

Step backwards, into Memory Lane
and see one's younger self again.
Revisit good old days once more
before you knock on Heaven's Door.

It's fun to capture times gone by
(it's true indeed the years do fly)
Reflecting on the happy / sad
weighing good against the bad.

That's life you see! A 'woe betide'.
Perhaps you'd like a slower stride?
Bet on chance; do or dare.
Exhale as if you've not a care.

When family's gone, and friends, and more
they'll live in albums from a drawer:
frequenting too your silent dreams;
or torturing in cruel extremes.

Do you yearn to halt that clock?

Embrace what's gone then seal that lock?

It ebbs away; too swift the tide.

Best buckle up, enjoy the ride.

"My Great-Aunt Rose"

My Great-Aunt came for tea today; the old girl's such a
hoot!
A genuine, real-life spinster, and a character, to boot!

We'll gather in a circle to hear all her golden tales.
And when, at last, her time is up our house erupts in wails.

She used to worked for MI5 - thus sworn to secrecy;
forsaking now those vows she tells of unheard history!

I'm far too patriotic so there's not much leaves my walls,
but Aunt Rose would be knighted . . if she'd been born with
balls.

Though this short tale I WILL reveal, cos credit where it's
due.
And you can make assumptions as to whether this is true.

She was 'friendly' with an artist who portrayed high
ranking folk.
He liked to paint their portraits - and include a personal
joke.

He painted Winston Churchill and a friendship there begun.
But unbeknown to Winston he had left his fly undone!

'Winnie' was a smoker and where his hand was placed,
on his lap, his fly undone . . a Corona cigar replaced!

When the masterpiece was finished, it just vanished? (so it's said!)
But I tell you now it isn't . . it's above my Great-Aunt's bed!

"Time to go"

I'm here my love, I'm with you. I'm here right by your side.
I don't think you can hear me now or see these tears I've cried.

I'll sit here 'til you leave me. My love, my life, my mate.
Take your time my darling. Let's make heaven wait.

Shall I sing 'our song' to you, the one you sang to me?
Shall I tell you one last time I love you endlessly?

Can you feel my old heart breaking? Or know the pain I feel.
Holding hands like this, my love, is horribly surreal.

How am I to carry on? Tell me how I'll breathe.
How am I to rise each day when filled with dread and grief?

Your breathing's getting shallow and I beg you to hold on.
Our daughter's driving over now, we need to be as one.

We're here my love, we're with you. It's time you be released.

Thank you for a lifetime - now darling rest in peace.

"Try to remember"

Do you remember, 60 years ago,
way back when we were young?
The belle o'the ball, the best of 'em all,
and I was fit an' strong.

Do you remember our four children?
All grown now, fled the nest.
They said we wouldn't last the course,
but hey, we passed the test.

I see you fed the dog again.
I fed her too, myself.
Did y'take your medication, Love?
cos it's still here on the shelf.

Shall we walk around the garden, dear?
Shall I make us both some tea?
I'll take a chair outside for you;
come . . and sit with me.

I'll remind you of the good old days;
we'll walk the Memory Mile.
Think of me as a 'friend' right now
as we reminisce a while.

Yes I DO remember Sally,
the doll you used to have.
Your brother, Bert, the sniper,
your sisters in the WRAF.

I'm glad your mum's still busy
baking cakes for your birthday 'do'.
I wish that I was young enough,
to be invited, too.

I know it's past your bedtime, dear.
Oh hush now, no more tears.
Of course I'll kneel and pray with you
as I've done for 60 years.

You don't remember who I am,
or all that we've lived through.
But rest assured my darling girl
. . I remember YOU!

"Nobody loves me . . "

I got no chocs nor roses and I didn't get a card.
I tried to wear a smile all day behind my fake facade.

I waited for the postman but alas he too drove by.
I came inside dejected, thinking "no one loves me, why?"

So I poured myself a glass of wine and pondered on my
past.
Thinking of my schooldays - and a boy from in my class.

I fancied him like mad back then, but we were just fifteen.
I was always nice to him; he was proper mean!

He used to tease me endlessly, made all the class join in.
He called me names, he pulled my hair, (sometimes I hated
him).

Then Billy got leukaemia and died within the year.
His mother mailed my valentine card, and still I have it
here.

See, even though he teased me so, Billy really cared.
(In front of other peers and pals, feelings can't be bared.)

Every year, this special day, I read those words he wrote.
And every time I do I get a lump inside my throat.

"I know you think I'm stupid cos I act so flippin' dumb,
but I really like you 'four eyes' - AND your big fat bum.
Some day I will marry you, I want to make you mine.
Can you guess who sent this card? Be my Valentine!"

False impression

Falsies are the trend these days. Noses, boobs, and bums.
Hair extensions. Knee replacements. Surgical flat new
tums.

I've endured a load of ops which cost an arm an' leg
('Dolly Parton' tits like these you can't buy "off-the-peg"!)

I'm almost quite addicted to my surgeon and his knife.
And every year my husband got a younger looking wife.

I had collagen in my creases and some lipo on my thighs.
I ditched designer glasses since I've laser-perfect eyes.

Acrylic nails with diamond studs shimmer in the sun.
I even got a piercing with my 'belly-button' done.

See, money was no problem, I've a shed load, truth be told.
All too pleased to pay the price to stop me looking old.

Tho the biggest dread I had to face was my own pearly whites.
(It's when the guy says 'open wide' .THAT just don't sit right!)

But I bit the bullet in the end and had the whole lot out!
Contemplating implants, but at forty grand a shout!?

Instead I got plain dentures which just proved I was an ass cos hubby's not been near me since he saw them in a glass.

And the worst dilemma of the lot was at my 'birthday do'.
Candles blown I laughed out loud; my 'teeth' grew wings and flew!

I've vowed this year to act my age, reveal myself less shady.
(I'm only truly grateful no-one sees my Tena Lady!)

Mother and Daughter

I KNOW I should visit my mother,
it's her 98th birthday, you see.
But it fills me with dread now, these visits:
That Home reeks of sadness, and wee.

I begged my son Tod, to come with me,
but he works every God hour he can.
He possesses no love nor the patience
to sit down and talk with his gran.

And these days my mum doesn't know us,
she stares into space, hours on end.
She looks so unkempt and bewildered.
This woman was once my best friend.

Oh to go back to the good days
when she mattered to me, and I, her.
She was beautiful, happy, and able:
but those good days are now just a blur.

Dad died when I was a nipper,
so forever twas just mum and me.
We were totally 'there' for each other.
My mum was the whole world to me.

I'm NOT going to visit tomorrow.
I'll go sometime soon: who can tell?
She'll not even notice my absence.
I'll take flowers, and chocolates as well.
....

Please dear, can you get my nice dress out?
And my hair? Can you make it look nice?
My daughter is coming tomorrow,
and I don't feel this look will suffice.

She'll be here for my 21st birthday,
she's bringing my grandson; young Tod.
He is so like my husband, his grandad.
Literally, Peas in a Pod!

Tod's 5; I remember his birth day.
Do you think we might go for a ride?
Oh I've not seen the seaside for ages.
Do you remember when I was a bride?

I think my dear husband is poorly,
he's not been to see me today.
He's perhaps making plans for our journey.
He says we're both going away.

Oh you've done up my hair really nicely!
And thanks for your caring my dear.
I'll sit here and wait her arrival.
My daughter. You watch. She'll be here.

"Blind as a daft bat"

I couldn't find my glasses - but I had them yesterday.
Believe me I searched everywhere; they must've 'walked away'.

I looked inside the rubbish and I scoured the ruddy house.
I never found my 'bins' but just a carcass of a mouse!

How on earth did that get there? My eyesight must be bad.
I buried it, I said a prayer, I really felt quite sad.

So I headed in to town today to get my eyesight tested.I
knew I'd have to walk cos if I drove, I'd be arrested!

Was hoping, NO! was praying, that I wouldn't meet a soul;
cos I couldn't see to wave hello, nor dare to cross the road!

I sat upon the chair and had to wait for my optician.
Relaying why I'm here today, excluding no omission.

He looked confused and then he said
"are these them'round your neck?"

Yep! There they are, upon a chain. I'm one pathetic wreck.

But it wasn't all a waste of time, I bought some contact lenses.
Blow the budget, what the heck. (I put it on expenses).

Then walking back to my abode, felt smug to tell the truth.
Missed the kerb, went headfirst, and broke my ruddy tooth!

"Losing it … all"

Oh the joys of getting older! Losing senses, youth, and mind.
I FEEL as if I'm young and yet my body's in decline.

I'm missing conversations cos I cannot hear a thing:
and my wardrobe's reminiscent of the days when I was thin.

I cannot see to sew these days, nor small-print in my books
and I've magnifying mirrors hanging everywhere, on hooks.

My gums recede and bleed and I've a denture in a glass.
My curly crowning glory too, has 'waved' farewell, alas.

Lace up shoes? Forget it, cos I can't bend down that far
(you should see me flippin' struggle getting in and out the car!)

I wouldn't blame the hubby if he chose to go 'astray'
cos no longer am I sexy in a black lace negligee!

I've wrinkles, batwings, facial hair; cellulite galore,
and I swear it won't be long before I knock on Heaven's Door.

I hate my gorgeous nieces. They're trendy, slim and young.
Nightclubs, parties, sexy guys: so much sin and FUN!

See? I'm a bitter, twisted moaner. An age-old thing, ya ken?
I need to find Nirvana cos I wanna be young again

"I love a man . . ."

Soldiers, sailors, 'boys in blue'.
Firemen, bandsmen, military too.
Anything less, to me's lukewarm.
A man is 'hot' in a uniform.

Smart an' dapper. Upper class.
Who wouldn't drool at a well-fit ass?
Men with a hefty wealthy ISA.
Armani wardrobes, even nicer.

Ballet dancers, under lights.
Bulging 'bits' in flesh-like tights.
(But NOT those sumo wrestlers! NO!
Too much blubber there on show.)

Even a Judge or politician,
gravedigger, oil rigger, or mortician!
A cashier guy scanning on a till ...
(Now a lifeguard bod . . . he would fit the bill!)

A boxer perhaps, or a circus clown.

One to lift up if the other knocked me down.

I admire skills of a craftsman's hands.

And the excellence of Olympians.

Oh hark at me, getting swept away!

(A dog's a better option any way)

See . . I don't need Sir Galahad;

cos the only MAN for me . . was Dad!

"Your turn next"

Oh laugh at me as I board the bus and struggle on each
stair.
Snigger with your buddies as I'm sorting out my fare.
You with your youth a'glowing and you think you know it
all.
Believe me dear, I've walked your walk and my life's been
a ball.

You see me as an 'old bird'. Well past my 'sell-by' date.
You class me as the walking dead with one foot in the
grave.
You think it's really funny that my memory's gone astray
and how I talk of bygone days like all was yesterday.

You roll your eyes when I relive the memories of my past.
I see you smirk and scoff with not a clue how life goes fast.
Cos your pathetic life revolves inside your mobile phone.
Texting all and sundry - from your bedroom, all alone.

Your beauty - there's no doubting. I was once like that.
Course you don't believe me, cos I talk in old folks' chat.
I think you call it Google, so check me out, on line.

© 2020 Lisa Talbott

You'll probably reconsider, once you see this past of mine.

I was a Prima Donna. Danced with the créme de la créme.
Revered, adored, respected. Back in my heyday then.
I bequeath my past to you my dear, by ode. NOT by text.
One day you might reach my age. Ah, the memories . . your
turn, next.

"Thank you for the memories"

Goodbye old buddy, farewell my friend.
I guess we're at our friendship's end.
All is tranquil. All's at ease.
Safe journey comrade; rest in peace.

Your pain's now gone, your worries too:
there's nothing left for you to do.
You fought but lost, what can I say?
We're born, we die . . life's just that way.

But oh the good times! What a blast.
Years of memories we amassed.
Remember on The Piste we skied?
We laughed until we almost wee'd.

Birthdays, Christmas, any time,
you'd turn up, with loads of wine.
We'd play 'our songs' and play them loud.
Just us two, no more allowed.

We never made it down the aisle

(though was an option for a while)

Great friendship our true destiny . . .

(Remember Blackpool, '83?!)

So here's to happy never after.

Boy, I'm gonna miss your laughter.

Visit me, if e're you can.

Thanks for my memories, you lovely man.

"Tick tock, tick tock"

Father Time has never been a friend of mine.
He never gives a soul a break.
Leaving anguish, heartache, in his wake.

He has no friends, nor ever tries to make amends.

No cares has he for what you feel.
He'll leave you wrecked. It's no big deal.

He stalks us all, both young and old.
He's fearless, brash. Unfeeling. Cold.

All he leaves is torment, strife, and memories of your better life.

He'll watch your sorrow: gleeful for a new tomorrow,
to cast his net and haul you in. Sickness, pain, and every sin.

You'll not elude Old Father Time. This hypocrite; this fake sublime.

So face him steadfast: stand your ground, brush him off and don't back down.

Getting old is his sadistic game.

And Mother Nature? She's the same.

"Let me go"

You've kept me in your 'memory box' for far too many
years.
I saw your fears, and watched you weep a million lonely
tears.

We talked about this often. We said you weren't to mourn.
You promised me, agreed with me, yet still you're there
forlorn.

And I watched you grieving daily. I felt your constant pain.
I tried to leave you signs to show that you can love again.

To have once more, what WE had. Journey forth, anew.
I saw it all, I felt it all, and lived it all - through you.

Yet here you are, still grieving. You broke your promise
Babe!
I know you hurt but begging you, our promise - don't
renege.

So please; put down your glass now. There's life outside your door.
Put on your smile. Live a while. It's not ME you're looking for.

And dance like no one's watching. Dance with a new love too.
And should sometime you hear 'our song' - know, I dance with you.

"Through a child's eyes"
A Short Story

I'm going to tell you a big secret, but you must promise NOT to tell a single soul! I mean it! If you do, I'm gonna deny all knowledge. And I'm going to have to 'unfriend' you, too; because my brother and I swore each other to secrecy! He FOUND fairies! Take that piece of knowledge in and digest it, will you?

I remember the day as clearly as having breakfast this morning. He was 7: and I know that he was 7 because he'd just had his 7th birthday party the day before. The day before he told me he'd found fairies. I can't even recall why it was ME he told. He was always closer to the youngest sister of our lot, but hey, I was pleased it WAS me! I was 13, and I SOOOO wanted to believe his 'fairy' tale.

Terry loved fishing. He was always down the brook with his fishing net in the summer. His birthday's in August. August 23rd. So on the 24th August, he'd taken his net and his jam jar, and his jam sandwiches too. Sticklebacks, minnows, and bullies his aim to net. Frogspawn too, sometimes! Yuk. Reminded me of school puddings.

Anyway. That was the day he saw them. Now being a 13 yr old girl I naturally assumed my brother's fairies would be the ethereal type. You know, the ones you'd see in the Cottingley book of fairies. Translucent wings, ballerina tutus, an acorn top for a hat! But they weren't Terry's fairies. Not at all! Not pixies, nor elves, or mini demons. His were miniature dwarf-like beings in a flying machine. One couldn't even blame his sightings on alcohol, he WAS only 7!

So desperate was he to make me believe he dragged me to where he'd spent his afternoon, fishing by the brook. We waited for two hours. He'd eaten his jam sandwiches hours before. And it was getting dusk. If we didn't get home before the lights came on, we'd be in trouble. So we went home.

My brother never spoke of his fairy tale again after that night. Who'd believe him? The whole family had a huge chuckle round the dinner table that night. Everyone laughed out loud. Terry didn't laugh. I didn't laugh.

Our family home went up for sale in the early 2000's. Everyone moved on; it was time to sell up and split the inheritance. A lifetime of memories to be discarded into some metal skip to become landfill. The new owners will never imagine the pure joys of us children hanging our Christmas stockings on that huge inglenook fireplace. They'll wonder why on earth the tin bath still hangs outside in the coal shed. How could they ever picture it being brought inside, filled with water that was heated on the range and then one after another we'd clean ourselves in it in front of a roaring fire. How they'd chuckle if they could see our mum putting rags in us girls' hair to make ringlets. And of our pets' cemetery too? What will do they with that? Whiskey, Janey, and Cilla are all buried there. We held ceremonies for them all.

It will all be 'modernised' and dehumanised. Our beloved memories erased like a bad smell. One last look round, to take stock of much happier days before I drop off the big old black key that opened to door to the heart of this home, and then it's goodbye.

I'll just double-check the attic... Everything's always been left to me, as usual, to finalise. And that's when I saw it! Right under the eaves tucked away so no sibling prying eyes would ever have found it. A shoe box. What can I say?? The most intricate, unique, perfect piece of indescribable imagery in the entire universe. A little "flying" machine? Inside, four miniature, perfectly formed, mummified, "dwarf-like fairies!"

I then remembered the day we found them… The day we swore each other to secrecy… Who would've believed

Part Ten: Last Words

No book is complete without a final chapter. An ending. Something that ties everything together. In short stories, it is where the conflict and plot are resolved. In longer works of fiction, the story ends – or the author sets up a possible sequel.

Poetry is unique, especially when a compendium covers such a wide variety of subjects. There is no "ending" or "resolution." Rather, the poet simply writes something that characterizes their thoughts as the book comes to a close.

In her typical style, Lisa managed to come up with just the right words to end the book. The final poem, "Picture it perfect," says a lot about the heart and soul of Lisa's poetry. When she sent it to me for inclusion in this book, I was immediately struck by how perfect it was for the final verse of "Weep and Wail."

"Picture it perfect"

I want to paint a picture but my paint has all gone dry.
I want to sing a song but find Soprano's far too high.
I tried to write a letter but my pen's right out of ink.
I need another lifetime to fulfil these thoughts I think.

I yearn to climb a mountain but the summit's always steep.
I'd love to swim with dolphins but I'm nervous of the
'deep'.
I dreamt of seeing icebergs but Antarctic's far too cold.
I wished I'd lived life differently. Now I'm much too old.

I'd build an animal sanctuary if I had my time again.
Loyalty unquestioned, as opposed to fellow man.
A place where nothing breathing would again encounter
harm.
Or perhaps a little country house where I could build a
farm.

So I'll paint a song with words and rhyme revealing how I feel.

Expressing all my thoughts and dreams to make my world surreal.

I'll paint my picture perfect. I'll let my heart reflect.

Or keep it all inside instead; just picture it perfect.

Acknowledgements

The most important person to acknowledge in "Weep and Wail" is Michael Paul Hurd for his friendship and professionalism in producing this book. He has worked tirelessly reading each one of my scripts, grouping them all together, and narrating each section. His advice and guidance has been invaluable, and I've learnt so much from him.

I'd also like to thank my greatest fan of all -- my wonderful mum, Elizabeth Talbott -- who never tires of being my first reader to check for any errors. If she laughs or cries, then I know I've written something to evoke an emotion.

Lisa Talbott

I'll reciprocate Lisa's acknowledgement. It has been a pleasure working with her through the production of this book. Collaboration, even when face-to-face, can be trying; the difficulty is compounded when there is an ocean and several time zones between us. Instead, we patiently worked through the challenges and came up with a cohesive book that I am proud to put my name on. I applaud Lisa for rising to the occasion, and especially for her quick turnaround on "My boob job," which was written in less than 24 hours after I asked Lisa to write it for my niece.

Second, I share Lisa's sentiment that no author can complete any of their works without the support of family members. I thank my wife, Sandy, for the love and support she has shown as I helped Lisa compile her poems and short stories into a cohesive production and for tolerating me working often late into the night to put this book together.

Michael Paul Hurd

Printed in Great Britain
by Amazon